DIRECT HITS

Core Vocabulary

Sixth Edition

For more information, please contact us by mail:

Direct Hits Publishing
2 The Prado, Unit 2, Atlanta GA 30309

Ted@DirectHitsPublishing.com

Or visit our website:
www.DirectHitsPublishing.com

Sixth Edition: June 2016

Despite our best efforts at editing and proofreading, the book may contain errors. Please feel free to contact us if you find an error, and any corrections can be found on our website.

ISBN: 978-1-936551-22-4

Written by Paget Hines
Edited by Ted Griffith
Cover Design by Carlo da Silva
Interior Design by Alison Rayner

Other Books by Direct Hits

Direct Hits Core Vocabulary is part of a larger series aimed at helping students improve their vocabulary. The series is designed as a progression to help students learn vocabulary as they get older, starting with *Direct Hits Essential Vocabulary*, then *Direct Hits Core Vocabulary*, and finally *Direct Hits Advanced Vocabulary*. Our books are available from Amazon, Barnes & Noble, and other major retailers.

For information on bulk orders, please email us at:
Ted@DirectHitsPublishing.com

ACKNOWLEDGEMENTS

This 6th edition reflects the collaborative efforts of an outstanding team of students, educators, reviewers, and project managers, each committed to helping young people attain their highest aspirations. Their insights and talents have been incorporated into *Direct Hits Core Vocabulary*.

I wish to express my gratitude to our Student Advisory Board: Tanner Hines, Kali Holliday, and Adam Liang. Their thoughtful input helped refine and update the book, keeping it readable and entertaining.

Judy Martinez was vital in the editing process. She combed each page to ensure that the grammar was consistent, and she helped me simplify and condense the examples when needed.

Alison Rayner was responsible for creating our interior design. I thank her not only for her creative talent, but also for her flexibility through multiple revisions.

Additionally, I am grateful to Carlo da Silva, who once again used his artistic and graphic skills to design our distinctive cover.

Direct Hits Core Vocabulary would not be possible without Claire Griffith. Her vision for Direct Hits guided every aspect of this book.

A big thank you goes out to Luther Griffith for his oversight and support. I appreciate his strong and practical guidance and organization.

A special thank you to Ted Griffith, who made sure that I stayed on task and kept me supplied with an abundance of my favorite coffee beans. As always, I thank my family for their patience and understanding as my work took over our dining room.

Paget Hines, Author

TABLE OF CONTENTS

INTRODUCTION

Why is vocabulary important, you ask?

Words are our tools for learning and communicating. A rich and varied vocabulary enables us to…

Speak more eloquently…

Describe more vividly…

Argue more compellingly…

Articulate more precisely…

Write more convincingly.

Research has proven that a powerful and vibrant vocabulary has a high correlation with success in school, business, the professions, and standardized tests including the PSAT, SAT, ACT, SSAT, and AP Exams. Yet many students complain that taking the ACT or SAT is like trying to understand a foreign language. They dread memorizing long lists of seemingly random words.

Their frustration is understandable.

Direct Hits Core Vocabulary offers a different approach. Each word is illustrated through relevant examples from popular movies, television, literature, music, historical events, and current headlines.

Students can place the words in a context they can easily understand and remember.

Building on the success of previous editions, the authors of *Direct Hits Core Vocabulary* have consulted secondary school teachers, tutors, parents, and students from around the world to ensure that these words and illustrations are exactly on target to prepare you for success on the SAT. You will find that the approach is accessible, effective, and even fun!

Direct Hits offers **selective** vocabulary using **relevant** examples with **vivid** presentation so you can achieve successful **results** on standardized tests and in life.

Let's get started!

HOW TO USE THIS BOOK

❶ The vocabulary word is always in bold print and capitalized.

❷ This is the word number, not the page number. All of the Direct Hits words are numbered in the order they appear in the Essential, Core, and Advanced books.

❸ When another Direct Hits vocabulary word is used, the word will be in bold print and capitalized. The word number (or book it is from) is inside the parentheses.

❹ The Pro Tip box is additional information to help expand your vocabulary knowledge.

❺ The example is written to show the vocabulary word in context.

❻ Prefix, Suffix, and/or Root box is a visual reference of word parts. The meaning is next to the word part(s) featured, and each box contains example words with definitions.

---

❷ 14 | **❶ EULOGY ❸**

*NOUN–A **LAUDATORY** (Word 202) speech or written tribute, especially one praising someone who has died*

❹ PRO TIP

EULOGY is often confused with **ELEGY**, which is a poem of lament and praise for the dead. **ELEGY** yields the tone words **ELEGIAC** or **ELEGIACAL**, which means sad or mournful.

EULOGY comes from the Greek prefix EU-, meaning "good" and the root LOGOS, meaning "word."

After Princess Diana died, her brother, Earl Spencer, gave a touching **EULOGY**, saying:

"*Diana was the very essence of compassion, of duty, of style, of beauty. All over the world she was a symbol of selfless humanity, a standard-bearer for the rights of the truly downtrodden, a truly British girl who transcended nationality, someone with a natural nobility who was classless, who proved in the last year that she needed no royal title to continue to generate her particular brand of magic.*"

❺ On the lighter side, in the movie *Zoolander*, Derek Zoolander delivered a **EULOGY** for his friends who died in the "Orange Mocha Frappuccino" gas fight.

❻

KNOW YOUR PREFIXES		
GREEK PREFIX:	**EULOGY**	a speech of praise
EU | good	**EUPHEMISM**	an inoffensive word substituted for an offensive one
	EUPHONY	a pleasing sound
	EUGENICS	the science of improving offspring
	EUPHORIA	a feeling of well-being, an almost excessive feeling of buoyant vigor and health
	EUTHANASIA	a method of causing a painless, peaceful death

CHAPTER 1

Rhetorical/Literary Terms

RHETORIC (Word 104) is the art of using words effectively in both speaking and writing, often in order to influence or persuade others. It is a term often used to describe the art of prose composition, and under its umbrella are many figures of speech.

You might think that literary terms such as **METAPHOR** (Word 3), **ANECDOTE** (Word 13), and **ALLUSION** (Word 15) are only useful in English class. NOT so. Rhetorical and literary terms show up in many places, even in our everyday lives. In this chapter we explore 16 terms that have frequently turned up on ACT, PSAT, SAT, and AP tests. Recognizing them will result in higher scores, but even better, using a variety of **RHETORICAL DEVICES** can enhance your writing and speaking and result in richer, more powerful, more effective expression.

1 | FIGURATIVE/METAPHORICAL LANGUAGE

*NOUN—A general term referring to language that describes a thing in terms of something else. The resemblance is **FIGURATIVE** (DH Essential), not **LITERAL** (DH Essential), as the reader is carried beyond the **LITERAL** meaning to consider the **NUANCES** (DH Advanced) and connotations of the words used in the comparison.*

METAPHOR can occur as a single comparison or as the central or controlling image of a whole poem or work. For instance:

"Whoso List to Hunt," a sonnet by the English poet Sir Thomas Wyatt (1503-1542), is **LITERALLY** about a man's **FUTILE** (Word 146) pursuit of an elusive deer. But it is usually seen as the tale of his fruitless wooing of an elusive woman, probably Anne Boleyn, who had married Henry VIII. The deer imagery of beauty, daintiness, and quickness **EVOKES** (Word 89) the characteristics of a woman and thus functions as the controlling **METAPHOR** of the poem.

There are many literary terms for different kinds of **METAPHORICAL** or **FIGURATIVE** language. Here are several of the most common.

2 | SIMILE

*NOUN—An explicit figure of speech that is a comparison between two essentially unlike things, usually using the words "like" or "as," which points out a **FIGURATIVE** (DH Essential) way that the two things ARE alike.*

One explicit comparison between two unlike things is from this first line of a romantic poem by William Wordsworth (1770-1850): "I wandered lonely as a cloud."

A person is NOT a cloud, but he is being likened to one in that he is floating aimlessly and solitarily across the landscape.

Some more examples of **SIMILES**:

"Death lies on her like an untimely frost.**"**

Juliet's father in Shakespeare's *Romeo and Juliet*

" *The apple-green car with the white vinyl roof and Florida plates turned into the street like a greased cobra.* **"**

Gloria Naylor's *The Women of Brewster Place*

" *Draw the stroke with grace, like a bird landing on the branch, not an executioner chopping off a devil's head.* **"**

Amy Tan's *The Bonesetter's Daughter*

3 | METAPHOR

NOUN—In its more narrow sense, a figure of speech in which one thing is described in terms of another using an implied comparison, without the use of "like" or "as."

Here is a line from Alfred Noyes's poem "The Highwayman": "The moon was a ghostly galleon tossed upon cloudy seas."

The moon is NOT a galleon (a large sailing ship from the 16th to 18th centuries), but in some respects it is LIKE a ship, and the clouds are LIKE waves. The omission of "like" or "as" makes the comparison strong and direct.

Some more examples of **METAPHORS**:

In the movie *The Dark Knight*, the Joker compares himself to a dog and a wrench when he tells Batman, "You know what I am? I'm a dog chasing cars. I wouldn't know what to do if I caught one. I'm a wrench in the gears."

In Shakespeare's *As You Like It*, the cynical Jacques gives his famous seven ages of man speech in which he compares the world to a stage, life to a play, and people to the actors:

" *All the world's a stage*
And all the men and women merely players:
They have their exits and their entrances;
And one man in his time plays many parts. **"**

4 | PERSONIFICATION

NOUN—A figure of speech in which an inanimate object is given human qualities or abilities

PERSONIFICATION is often used in literary works to enhance the mood or power of an image. In "I Wandered Lonely as a Cloud," Wordsworth describes a "host of golden daffodils" on the hillside beside the lake, giving them human actions and emotions with which he can identify:

> *"The waves beside them danced; but they*
> *Outdid the sparkling waves in glee."*

Advertising slogans also utilize **PERSONIFICATION**. Goldfish crackers are "the snack that smiles back."

5 | PARALLELISM/PARALLEL STRUCTURE

NOUN—A rhetorical device or sentence construction which involves using matching grammatical patterns to establish the equivalent relationship or importance of two or more items. PARALLELISM provides balance and AUTHORITY (DH Essential) to sentences.

Charles Dickens's novels are full of rich **PARALLELISM**. Here is one example from the novel *Great Expectations*, with part of the young boy Pip's description of the "fearful man" he has encountered:

> *"A man <u>with no hat</u>, and <u>with broken shoes</u>, and <u>with an old rag</u> tied round his head. A man who had been <u>soaked</u> in water, and <u>smothered</u> in mud, and <u>lamed</u> by stones, and <u>cut</u> by flints, and <u>stung</u> by nettles, and <u>torn</u> by briars; who <u>limped</u>, and <u>shivered</u>, and <u>glared</u> and <u>growled</u>; and whose teeth <u>chattered</u> in his head as he <u>seized</u> me by the chin."*

Here is an illustration of a sentence where **PARALLEL STRUCTURE** is used in two places:

PARALLEL STRUCTURE

> **"**Early to bed and early to rise makes a man
> healthy, wealthy, and wise.**"**
>
> Benjamin Franklin

early to bed }
early to rise }   *makes a man*   { healthy
                                                  { wealthy
                                                  { and wise

More examples are:

"Shane was torn between <u>achieving</u> his goal of forgetting his past and starting a new life or <u>saving</u> his friends in the valley."

Note that both ideas are expressed with the "-ing" form of the verbs.

"Lies are usually told <u>to protect</u> the teller and <u>to deceive</u> the listener." Note the repetition of the "to" in the infinitive form of the **PARALLEL** ideas.

6 | IRONIC

ADJECTIVE—Using words to convey a meaning that is the opposite of its literal meaning

IRONICALLY

ADVERB—Pertaining to, exhibiting, or characterized by mockery

PRO TIP

LITERARY **IRONY** is a figure of speech in which what we say or write conveys the opposite of its literal meaning.

SITUATIONAL **IRONY** is when there is an incongruity between the actual result of a sequence of events and the normal or expected result.

IRONY (DH Essential) involves the perception that things are not what they are said to be or what they seem.

Here are some examples of **IRONY**:

In *Star Wars*, Han Solo tells Jabba the Hutt, "Jabba, you're a wonderful human being." Jabba is, in fact, neither wonderful nor a human being!

In Shakespeare's *Julius Caesar*, Marc Antony gives a famous **IRONIC** speech in which he repeats "And Brutus is an honorable man," when Brutus has just killed Julius Caesar and is not honorable at all!

In Sophocles's *Oedipus Rex* it is **IRONIC** that Oedipus thinks he is the detective in finding out who killed his predecessor, when he is actually, **IRONICALLY**, the murderer.

For situational **IRONY**: In 1912 the Titanic was proclaimed to be "100 percent unsinkable," yet it sank on its maiden voyage.

An important note: Alanis Morrisette's song "Ironic" is actually devoid of true examples of **IRONY**; they are just unfortunate situations. That, in and of itself, is **IRONIC**!

7 | SYNOPSIS

NOUN—A brief summary of the major points of a thesis, theory, story, or literary work; an abstract

Have you ever been asked to summarize a movie, television show, or a YouTube clip? If so, you would have provided a **SYNOPSIS** or brief summary. Here is a **SYNOPSIS** of the the HBO series *Game of Thrones*: Set in the fictitious land of Westeros, nine families battle for control of the Iron Throne. Civil War breaks out as the descendants of past kings and lords battle for power. While this struggle wages in the kingdom, problems north of The Wall emerge. The Wildlings seek to take advantage of the political turmoil and conquer the lands to the south. All of the conflict is further complicated by mythical powers and magic forces that no one person can control, including the army of undead heading toward The Wall and the Kingdom of Westeros.

8 | SATIRE, LAMPOON, PARODY

NOUN—A work that ridicules human vices, follies, and foibles; comic criticism.

SATIRIZE, LAMPOON, PARODY

VERB—To ridicule or mock, often **SARCASTICALLY** *(DH Essential)*

The ancient Greek playwright Aristophanes mastered the art of using **SATIRE** to mock public figures. In his play *The Clouds*, Aristophanes **LAMPOONS** Socrates as an abstract philosopher who operates a "Thinking Shop." Perched in a basket suspended from the ceiling, Socrates teaches his students how to prove anything, even if it is false.

Many centuries later, *Saturday Night Live* is still using **SATIRE** to mock public figures and expose their foibles. *SNL* skits frequently are **PARODIES** of political speeches and debates, meant to **SATIRIZE** political figures. The *SNL* cast members are famous for their **PARODIES** of celebrities. Tina Fey **SATIRIZED** Sarah Palin, Andy Samberg often **LAMPOONED** actor Nicholas Cage, and Will Ferrell played Alex Trebek in *SNL's Celebrity Jeopardy* **PARODIES**.

9 | HYPERBOLE

NOUN—A figure of speech in which exaggeration is used for emphasis or effect; extreme exaggeration

Have you ever exaggerated something to make a point? We all do, often for comic effect. In show business these exaggerations are called hype. In literature and daily life they are called **HYPERBOLES**. Here are some commonly used **HYPERBOLES**:

"I'm so tired I could sleep for a year."
"I'm so hungry I could eat a horse."
"This book weighs a ton."

<u>From poetry:</u>

"I'll love you, dear, I'll love you
Till China and Africa meet,
And the river jumps over the mountain
And the salmon sing in the street,
I'll love you till the ocean
Is folded and hung up to dry
And the seven stars go squawking
Like geese about the sky"

From "As I Walked Out One Evening" by W. H. Auden

<u>From literature:</u>

"A day was twenty-four hours long but seemed longer. There was no hurry, for there was nowhere to go, nothing to buy and no money to buy it with, nothing to see outside the boundaries of Maycomb County."

From *To Kill A Mockingbird* by Harper Lee

10 | CARICATURE

NOUN—Visual art or descriptive writing that deliberately exaggerates distinctive features or peculiarities of a subject for comic or absurd effect

Do you look at the editorial cartoons in your local newspaper? Editorial cartoonists often incorporate **CARICATURES** of political figures into their cartoons. **CARICATURES** can be about physical features or about controversial topics such as economic policies, war, or healthcare, to name a few. For example, Thomas Nast's **CARICATURES** of Boss Tweed depicted him as a vulture, helping to focus public attention on the Tweed Ring's corrupt practices in 19th century politics in New York City. Some of the most common political cartoons have been of U.S. Presidents. President Barack Obama's exaggerated features include a large toothy smile with a pointed chin and big ears.

11 | EPIC

NOUN—A long narrative poem written in a grand style to celebrate the feats of a legendary hero
ADJECTIVE—Grand, sweeping, or of historical or legendary importance

SAGA

NOUN—A long narrative story; a heroic tale

Both **EPICS** and **SAGAS** are long and feature the feats of heroes. The two literary forms differ in that an **EPIC** is a narrative poem and a **SAGA** is a narrative story written in prose.

Homer's *Iliad* is the first and arguably the best **EPIC** in Western literature. Other famous **EPICS** include Virgil's *Aeneid*, Homer's *The Odyssey*, and Milton's *Paradise Lost*. J. K. Rowling's series of seven Harry Potter novels provides a contemporary example of a literary **SAGA**, while George Lucas's six Star Wars films provide a contemporary example of a cinematic **SAGA**.

12 | FORESHADOWING

*VERB—A suggestion or indication that something will happen in a story; a hint that **PRESAGES** (DH Advanced)*

The conclusion of *Batman Begins* **FORESHADOWS** the caped crusader's coming battle with the Joker. As the film ends, Lieutenant Gordon unveils a Bat-Signal for Batman. He then mentions a criminal who, like Batman, has "a taste for the theatrical," leaving a Joker card at his crime scenes. Batman promises to investigate, thus **FORESHADOWING** his coming confrontation with the Joker in *The Dark Knight*. Similarly, *The Dark Knight Rises* teasingly ends with **FORESHADOWING**. At the end of the film, John Blake reveals that his first name is Robin and inherits the Bat Cave. Could this **FORESHADOW** future Batman films?

13 | ANECDOTE

NOUN—A short account of an interesting or humorous incident

PRO TIP

ANECDOTAL, the adjective form of **ANECDOTE**, has become a somewhat negative word applied to an attempt to support an opinion with only an isolated or personal example based on casual or informal observations. Others would reject **ANECDOTAL** evidence as too slim and unscientific to be persuasive.

World-renowned physicist Albert Einstein and Anthony Kiedis, the lead singer of the Red Hot Chili Peppers, were both very good at telling interesting **ANECDOTES**.

Einstein was often asked to explain the general theory of relativity. "Put your hand on a hot stove for a minute, and it seems like an hour," he once declared. "Sit with a pretty girl for an hour, and it seems like a minute. That's relativity."

An **ANECDOTE** Anthony Kiedis told about being the opening act for the Rolling Stones:

“*Opening for the Stones is a crummy job...First you get there and they won't let you do a sound check. Then they give you an eightieth of the stage. They set aside this tiny area and say, 'This is for you. You don't get the lights, and you're not allowed to use our sound system. And oh, by the way, you see that wooden floor? That's Mick's imported antique wood flooring from the Brazilian jungle, and that's what he dances on. If you so much as look at it, you won't get paid.'*”

14 | EULOGY

*NOUN—A **LAUDATORY** (Word 202) speech or written tribute, especially one praising someone who has died*

EULOGY comes from the Greek prefix EU-, meaning "good" and the root LOGOS, meaning "word."

After Princess Diana died, her brother, Earl Spencer, gave a touching **EULOGY**, saying:

"*Diana was the very essence of compassion, of duty, of style, of beauty. All over the world she was a symbol of selfless humanity, a standard-bearer for the rights of the truly downtrodden, a truly British girl who transcended nationality, someone with a natural nobility who was classless, who proved in the last year that she needed no royal title to continue to generate her particular brand of magic.*"

On the lighter side, in the movie *Zoolander*, Derek Zoolander delivered a **EULOGY** for his friends who died in the "Orange Mocha Frappuccino" gas fight.

KNOW YOUR PREFIXES

GREEK PREFIX:		
EU | good	**EULOGY**	a speech of praise
	EUPHEMISM	an inoffensive word substituted for an offensive one
	EUPHONY	a pleasing sound
	EUGENICS	the science of improving offspring
	EUPHORIA	a feeling of well-being, an almost excessive feeling of buoyant vigor and health
	EUTHANASIA	a method of causing a painless, peaceful death

15 | ALLUSION

NOUN—An indirect or brief reference to a person, event, place, phrase, piece of art, or literary work that assumes a common knowledge with the reader or listener

Many contemporary songs and TV shows contain clever **ALLUSIONS** to works of literature. For example, in her song "Love Story," Taylor Swift **ALLUDES** to Shakespeare's play *Romeo and Juliet* and Hawthorne's novel *The Scarlet Letter* when she warns her romantic lover, "Cause you were Romeo, I was a scarlet letter."

The TV show *Pretty Little Liars* often uses literary **ALLUSIONS** in the titles of its episodes. For example, the *Pretty Little Liars* episode "To Kill a Mocking Girl" **ALLUDES** to Harper Lee's novel *To Kill a Mockingbird*. In the show, when the girls investigate the murder of their **ENIGMATIC** (Word 125) friend Alison, they discover that Alison had a secret alternate identity: Vivian Darkbloom. This is an **ALLUSION** to Vladimir Nabokov's *Lolita*, as Vivian Darkbloom, who appears as a minor character in the novel, is an anagram of the author's name.

16 | ANALOGY

NOUN—A similarity or likeness between things—events, ideas, actions, trends—that are otherwise unrelated

ANALOGOUS

ADJECTIVE—Comparable or similar in certain respects

Did you know that for most of its history the SAT included a number of **ANALOGY** questions? For example, students were asked to see the **ANALOGY** or similarity between a tree and a forest and a star and a galaxy. The **ANALOGY** is that a tree is part of a forest in the same way that a star is part of a galaxy. Although the College Board removed analogies in 2005, SAT test writers still expect students to recognize **ANALOGIES** in critical readings. Don't be confused by the phrase "is most **ANALOGOUS** to." The question is asking you to identify a situation or example that is most similar to the one in the reading passage.

CHAPTER 1 REVIEW

Use the word bank below to help complete the sentences. NOT all the words are used! The answer key is on page 142.

Word Bank:

allusion	analogy	eulogy
foreshadowing	hyperbole	metaphor
personification	saga	satire
synopsis		

1. Shows like *The Daily Show*, *Last Week Tonight*, and *Saturday Night Live* are known for politcal _____. All these shows use humor to critique current events.

2. Many people feel that a funeral brings closure to the loved ones of the deceased. The _____ is usually given by relatives and close friends. The aim is to share memories and hopefully make people feel a little better about the loss.

3. The teacher had to remind the student about the danger of too much exaggeration. While _____ can be used in an essay, it should be done so only to underscore an important point.

4. The _____ of the stranded hikers was terrifying. It was a miracle that they survived so many days in the wilderness with virtually no food or water. Rescuers could not believe that the survivors had lived through a lightning storm and a record-breaking heat wave.

5. The friend wanted a _____ of the *The Walking Dead*, but he did not want any spoilers to be revealed because he planned on watching the series on Netflix over the winter break.

CHAPTER 2

Name That Tone/ Watch That Attitude

On every PSAT, SAT, ACT, and AP English exam there are questions that ask about an author's ATTITUDE, the author's or speaker's TONE, or the MOOD of a passage. The attitude, tone, or mood can be identified by examining the language and word choices in a passage. One way to think about TONE is that it is very akin to TONE OF VOICE.

To determine the tone of a passage, you may find these steps helpful:

1. Underline the descriptive words in the passage. These can be adjectives, adverbs, verbs, and nouns.
2. Identify the connotations of these words. Are they positive or negative? Or perhaps neutral?
3. Characterize the feelings the connotations generate.
4. Decide if there are hints that the speaker may not really mean everything he or she says. Such **NUANCES** (DH Advanced) might lead you to identify an **IRONIC** (Word 6) tone.
5. Visualize the expression on the speaker's face, for instance a **WRY** (Word 86) smile or a contemptuous smirk.
6. Listen to the passage. What is the author's TONE OF VOICE?

In addition to the tone words you have already encountered, like **AMBIVALENT** (Word 167), **SARCASTIC** (DH Essential), and **NOSTALGIC** (Word 178), we have included 20 additional tone words that have appeared on recent tests.

17 | WISTFUL

*ADJECTIVE—Longing and yearning, tinged with **MELANCHOLY** (DH Essential) and **PENSIVENESS** (Word 25)*

It is not uncommon for parents and their kids to have very different feelings about heading off to college. Typically, college-bound students are anxious and excited about leaving home and starting life on campus. Parents, on the other hand, become quite **WISTFUL** when their children graduate high school and leave for college. While they are proud of their child's achievements, they are sad that the days of having a child at home are gone.

18 | EARNEST, SINCERE

ADJECTIVE—Serious in intention or purpose; showing depth and genuine feelings

Adele wrote her song "Rolling in the Deep" on the same day she broke up with her boyfriend. The lyrics display Adele's **SINCERE** belief that their relationship could have been very special.

"*We could have had it all
Rolling in the deep
You had my heart inside of your hand
And you played it to the beat*"

When asked how she felt about her breakup, Adele did not sugarcoat the truth. She spoke **EARNESTLY**: "I was really, really angry with my personal life up to about a year ago. I've grown up a little as well, and I like to think I've blossomed into who I'm going to become."

Adele certainly did move on successfully and "Rolling in the Deep" became her first #1 hit!

19 | DISGRUNTLED, DISCONTENTED

ADJECTIVE—Angry; dissatisfied; annoyed; impatient; irritated

Some of the top companies in the world work tirelessly to make sure that their employees are not **DISGRUNTLED**. After all, happy employees are more productive than **DISCONTENTED** employees. Google is exceptionally notable for the benefits it provides its employees. At the Googleplex office in Mountain View, California, employees bring their pets to work, receive complimentary gourmet meals, have gym and pool access, and much more. It is clear that Google doesn't want its employees to be **DISGRUNTLED**.

20 | AUTHORITATIVE

*ADJECTIVE—Commanding and self-confident; likely to be respected and obeyed, based on competent **AUTHORITY** (DH Essential)*

In *The Walking Dead*, Rick Grimes becomes the **AUTHORITATIVE** leader of a group of survivors living in the time of a zombie apocalypse **PANDEMIC** (Word 148). Rick's group faces **PERILOUS** (Word 84) situations where they must kill in order to survive. **IRONICALLY** (Word 6), Rick and his fellow survivors face more danger from other humans than they do from the zombies aimlessly wandering the streets and countryside. Rick's **AUTHORITATIVE** manner inspires those around him to fight for their life and work for a better life.

21 | FRIVOLITY

*NOUN—The trait of being **FRIVOLOUS**; not serious or sensible*

FRIVOLOUS

ADJECTIVE—Lacking any serious purpose or value; given to trifling or levity

One form of **FRIVOLOUS** spending that has become **UBIQUITOUS** (Word 185) is bottled water. Many bottled water companies simply sell municipal water; you can get the same water from your tap. Also, if not properly recycled, disposable water bottles contribute to **FRIVOLOUS** waste. The 30 billion plastic water bottles that are thrown away each year can take thousands of years to decompose. Using a reusable water bottle or canteen reduces **FRIVOLOUS** consumption, saves money, and protects the environment.

22 | ACERBIC, ACRID
ADJECTIVE—Harsh, bitter, sharp, CAUSTIC (DH Advanced)

ACERBIC and **ACRID** both refer to the sharp and corrosive tone displayed by acid-tongued critics. **ACRID** can also refer to an unpleasantly sharp smell or taste. *House of Cards*'s main character, Francis Underwood, is famous for his **ACERBIC** comments directed at everyone around him, including the audience. In one episode, he tells the camera after the Russian president kisses his wife, "I'd push him down the stairs and light his body on fire just to watch it burn if it wouldn't start a world war." As much as Underwood is offended that the Russian president publicly kissed his wife, Francis is most upset that it makes him look weak in front of his D.C. colleagues.

Charles McGrath wrote in the *New York Times* that Gore Vidal, "the novelist, essayist, screenwriter, and all-around man of letters who died in July at the age of 86...was shown in several clips from a PBS documentary being his usual **ACERBIC**, witty and elegant self: taking America to task for needless wars, a bloated military-industrial complex, and political hypocrisy."

23 | SOLEMN, SOMBER
ADJECTIVE—Not cheerful or smiling; serious; gloomy;
GRAVE (DH Essential)

January 10, 2016, when David Bowie died, marked a **SOMBER** day for the entire world. Bowie was regarded by many as a legendary artist and rock and roll chameleon. Bowie's **INNOVATIVE** (Word 164) musical style influenced artists spanning all modern genres. His death was especially **SOLEMN** because it came as a shock to fans and just days after the release of his final studio album, *Blackstar*.

24 | INQUISITIVE
ADJECTIVE—Curious; inquiring

A common experiment in high school physics class is the egg drop. The experiment applies Newton's Laws, as well as the first law of thermodynamics, because it tests the laws of inertia, gravity, drag, kinetic energy, and impact. Students are asked how best to design a crumple zone to protect the egg from cracking. **INQUISITIVE** students will often research designs ahead of time online and ask the teacher about the most successful builds from previous years.

25 | REFLECTIVE, PENSIVE
*ADJECTIVE—Engaged in, involving, or reflecting deep or serious thought, usually marked by sadness or **MELANCHOLY** (DH Essential)*

The Thinker, a famous bronze and marble sculpture by August Rodin, depicts a **PENSIVE** man, that is, one captured in deep thought. The pose of *The Thinker,* seated with one fist nestled under his chin, has become very famous. The pose of deep **REFLECTION** has led many to believe that the man is struggling with some form of internal conflict. The original sculpture is located in Paris, but there are dozens of authentic cast replicas all over the world, including 13 in North America.

26 | EQUIVOCAL
*ADJECTIVE—**AMBIGUOUS** (Word 176), open to interpretation, having several equally possible meanings*

EQUIVOCATE
*VERB—To avoid making an explicit statement; to hedge; to use vague or **AMBIGUOUS** (see KNOW YOUR ROOTS, p. 102) language*

The classic movie *The Graduate* has a particularly **EQUIVOCAL** ending. Ben Braddock storms the church to stop Elaine Robinson's wedding but arrives just after the vows are said. Nonetheless, the newlywed Elaine sees Ben and decides to run off with him. Laughing, the couple race out of the church and board a bus. But then their smiles fade, and they become strangely silent. The film's **AMBIGUOUS** ending leaves the audience wondering if they really love each other and what will happen to them in the future.

In election campaigns, candidates often appear to be **EQUIVOCATING**, as if fearful of losing votes by coming out too **UNEQUIVOCALLY** on one side or another of an issue.

Alfred Hitchcock **COINED** (DH Advanced) the term of what is now a commonly used plot device in movies: the MacGuffin. A MacGuffin is a critically important object that drives the story forward, but whose exact nature usually remains **AMBIGUOUS** and undefined. In the film *Citizen Kane*, the meaning of the word "Rosebud" is the MacGuffin. In the movie *Pulp Fiction*, the briefcase is an **EQUIVOCAL** MacGuffin. The briefcase is very important to the characters, yet we never see the contents of the precious luggage. Fans of the movie often hypothesize and debate about the **AMBIGUOUS** contents of the briefcase.

27 | DEFERENTIAL
ADJECTIVE—Respectful; dutiful

That Prince William's wife, Kate Middleton, Duchess of Cambridge and future queen of England, is a former commoner means that she must show proper **DEFERENCE** to the royal family, including Princesses Beatrice and Eugenie, the daughters of Prince Andrew. This **DEFERENTIAL** protocol is outlined in the "Order Of Precedence Of The Royal Family," which was recently revised by Queen Elizabeth to take into account Kate's non-royal origins.

On the hit Masterpiece Theater TV show *Downton Abbey*, the valet Bates must show proper **DEFERENCE** to Lord Grantham, even though the two served together in the Boer war. In the highly hierarchal world of early 20th century British society, his role as a servant requires that he be **DEFERENTIAL**.

28 | EBULLIENT, EUPHORIC

ADJECTIVE—Feeling or expressing great happiness or triumph; elated

> **PRO TIP**
>
> The word **EBULLIENT** comes from the Latin verb *ebullire*, to bubble forth or be boisterous, going back to *bullire*, to boil. So an **EBULLIENT** person is bubbly, upbeat, and high-spirited.

The London Olympics Women's Soccer final was a **EUPHORIC** day for the U.S. team. The Americans won the gold medal against Japan and avenged their defeat in the 2011 FIFA Women's World Cup final. The American team was elated to win the third consecutive Olympic gold medal for the United States.

Even though the Japanese women were **DOWNCAST** (DH Essential) at the end of the final game; they were **EBULLIENT** as they stood on the medal stand to receive their Olympic silver medals. (They also got to fly home in business class). The Canadian women's team was **ECSTATIC** (DH Essential) when they received their bronze medals since they were the first Canadian team sport to bring back a medal since the 1936 Berlin Olympic games.

29 | MALEVOLENT

ADJECTIVE—Wishing evil to others, showing ill will

BENEVOLENT *(DH Essential)*

ADJECTIVE—Well-meaning; kindly

Mother Teresa was a **BENEVOLENT** Catholic nun who served the people of India for over 45 years, ministering to the poor, sick, and orphaned, while spreading a message of love. Mother Teresa also founded a program called Missionaries of Charity, which supported soup kitchens, orphanages, schools, and homes for people with HIV/AIDS. Mother Teresa's **BENEVOLENCE** can be noted in such sayings as:

"*Love is a fruit in season at all times, and within reach of every hand.***"**

Perhaps the most **MALEVOLENT** of all historical figures was Hitler, who ordered the deaths of millions of people during the Holocaust.

In Shakespeare's *Othello*, Iago **MALEVOLENTLY** manipulates Othello into believing that his loving and innocent wife, Desdemona, is unfaithful. The question of Iago's motives remains one of the most mysterious of literary enigmas. Perhaps he is simply evil.

30 | WHIMSICAL

ADJECTIVE—Playful; fanciful; CAPRICIOUS (Word 195); given to whimsies or odd notions

In Disney/Pixar's *Up*, Carl Fredricksen lives in a quirky old house painted in lots of bright colors surrounded by modern, sleek skyscrapers. His multicolored cottage adds a touch of **WHIMSY** to the sterility of the neighborhood. His unique house becomes even more **WHIMSICAL** when he ties it to thousands of colorful balloons and flies it through town. The citizens are delighted by the fanciful flying house.

31 | PROSAIC, MUNDANE

ADJECTIVE—Dull; uninteresting; ordinary; commonplace; tedious; PEDESTRIAN (DH Advanced); VAPID (DH Advanced); BANAL (Word 121); HACKNEYED (DH Advanced); unexceptional

Originally, **PROSAIC** simply referred to PROSE, writing that was not POETRY. It referred to more factual, unimaginative writing, having the character and form of PROSE. Then, it did not have negative **NUANCES** (DH Advanced), but it has now come to be used almost always in a **DISPARAGING** (Word 203) sense.

You might refer to your tedious, unglamorous job as **PROSAIC** or to the **MUNDANE** monotony of your **PROSAIC** life or to the unhelpful, **HACKNEYED** (DH Advanced) nature of someone's **PROSAIC** advice. If you are an F. Scott Fitzgerald fan, you might want to label Ernest Hemingway's simple, straightforward prose style as **PROSAIC** but Fitzgerald's more lyrical prose style as **POETIC**.

32 | VITRIOLIC

ADJECTIVE—Bitter; **CAUSTIC** *(DH Advanced);* **ACERBIC** *(Word 22); filled with malice*

The 2016 presidential primary season was historic for many reasons. One example that illustrates the **HYSTERIA** (DH Essential) of the voters' passions is the rallies for Donald Trump. His fame as a reality television show star and reputation as a businessman made him popular with droves of politically disillusioned people. Trump's **PENCHANT** (Word 194) for politically incorrect speeches fueled **VITRIOLIC** behavior among his fans. At one rally in North Carolina, a Trump supporter punched a protester in the face. Passions have been equally strong amongst supporters for Bernie Sanders, but the rallies for Sanders have not become violent.

33 | CONCILIATORY

ADJECTIVE—Appeasing; intending to **PLACATE** *(DH Advanced)*

Prior to the rise of Donald Trump in the 2016 Republican primary, Jeb Bush was the presumptive Republican nominee for most political **PUNDITS** (Word 206) as early as 2012. Shockingly, Jeb Bush was unable to win a single primary or caucus; he only garnered 8% of the vote in South Carolina. Jeb Bush suspended his campaign. In his **CONCILIATORY** speech, Jeb acknowledged that the primary race had presented more challenges than he expected. He apologized to his supporters that he had not been able to be more successful and thanked them for their belief in him.

34 | DESPAIRING

ADJECTIVE—Showing the loss of all hope

After the stock market crash of 1929, the majority of the American public was **DESPAIRING**. One author described the general public emotion as "fear mixed with a **VERTIGINOUS** [DH Advanced] disorientation." So many had lost their life savings and were thrust into a life of poverty. The feelings of **DESPAIR** only increased throughout the 12-year-long Great Depression, which concluded with the American mobilization for World War II.

35 | INFLAMMATORY

ADJECTIVE—Arousing; intended to inflame a situation or ignite angry or violent feelings

Are you familiar with the online practice of "trolling"? *PC* magazine defines a troll as an online user who posts **INFLAMMATORY** and disrespectful remarks simply to stimulate emotions. For example, a troll might visit a YouTube video regarding the latest Mac release and post an **INFLAMMATORY** remark about Apple computers just to provoke angry responses.

INFLAMMATORY RHETORIC (Word 104) has become pervasive in political debates over such **PARTISAN** (Word 159) issues as abortion, illegal immigration, healthcare, and raising or lowering taxes.

36 | NONCHALANT

ADJECTIVE—Having an air of casual indifference; coolly unconcerned

When you are driving, do you slow down for a yellow light and promptly stop for a red light? We hope so. While careful and law-abiding drivers follow these rules of the road, not all drivers do. Italian drivers are famous for their **NONCHALANT** attitude toward yellow and even red lights. One typical Italian cab driver **NONCHALANTLY** explained that lights are merely advisory: "Everyone drives through yellow lights and fresh red ones. It is no big deal." Needless to say, we hope you will not take such a **NONCHALANT** attitude.

CHAPTER 2 REVIEW

Use the word bank below. The answer key is on page 142.

Word Bank:

acerbic	disgruntled	despairing	ecstatic
inquisitive	mundane	solemn	wistful

Word: _____

Definition in your own words:

_____

Word: _____

Definition in your own words:

_____

Word: _____

Draw it:

Word: _____

Draw it:

Word: _____

Use the word in a sentence that helps explain what it means.

_____

_____

Word: _____

Use the word in a sentence that helps explain what it means.

_____

_____

Word: _____

Use the word in a sentence that helps explain what it means.

_____

_____

Word: _____

Use the word in a sentence that helps explain what it means.

_____

_____

CHAPTER 3

Let's Break it Down!

A prefix and/or suffix is a meaningful element added to a root in order to direct or change the root's meaning.

A prefix is a word part placed before a root. Prefixes are short but mighty. A knowledge of prefixes can help you unlock the meaning of difficult words. Many vocabulary books contain long lists of Latin and Greek prefixes. Many like ANTI (against), SUB (under), and MULTI (many) are well-known and obvious. Still others, like PERI (around), generate few, if any, words tested on the PSAT, SAT, and ACT. This chapter will focus on five sets of the most widely-used prefixes on standarized tests.

A suffix is a word part that is added to the end of a root or word. We are including in this chapter a number of words ending with the suffix -OUS, by far the most useful suffix on any standardized test.

A. *E* AND *EX*: THE MIGHTY PREFIXES *E* AND *EX* TELL YOU THAT THINGS ARE GOING OUT

The prefixes *E* and *EX* are **UBIQUITOUS** (Word 185). You are familiar with them in everyday words such as EXIT, EXTINGUISH, and ERASE. The prefixes *E* and *EX* always mean OUT. Here are seven frequently tested words that begin with the prefixes *E* and *EX*:

37 | EXPUNGE, EXCISE, EXPURGATE

VERB—To take OUT; to delete; to remove

In the movie *300*, Xerxes threatened to **EXPUNGE** all memory of Sparta and Leonidas: "Every piece of Greek parchment shall be burned, every Greek historian and every Greek scribe shall have his eyes put out and his thumbs cut off. Ultimately the very name of Sparta or Leonidas will be punishable by death. The world will never know you existed."

Xerxes failed to carry out his threat to **EXCISE** the names of Sparta and King Leonidas from the historic record. However, a powerful Egyptian Pharaoh, Thutmose III, did succeed in **EXPURGATING** the name of his stepmother, Hatshepsut, from Egyptian monuments. A female pharaoh, Hatshepsut reigned for nearly 20 years in the 15th century BC. Possibly motivated by jealousy, Thutmose ruthlessly defaced his stepmother's monuments and **EXPURGATED** her name from historic records. All memory of Hatshepsut was lost until 19th century Egyptologists rediscovered her monuments and restored her place in history.

38 | ECCENTRIC

ADJECTIVE—Literally OUT of the center; departing from a recognized, conventional, or established norm; an odd, UNCONVENTIONAL (Word 171) person

There are many **INFAMOUS** (DH Essential) and odd celebrities and billionaires known for their bizarre behavior; however, Howard Hughes is remembered for his **ECCENTRIC** actions. In 2004, Leonardo DiCaprio portrayed Hughes in *The Aviator*. This film depicted some of Hughes's

UNCONVENTIONAL (Word 171) antics. Despite being a billionaire, Hughes became a paranoid **RECLUSE** (Word 139). For the remainder of his life, Hughes locked himself away in various hotel rooms all over the world. At times, his diet consisted of only chicken and milk. He would relieve himself in empty food containers. When he died in 1976, Hughes was **EMACIATED** (DH Essential) and unrecognizable.

39 | EXTRICATE

VERB—To get OUT of a difficult situation or entanglement

EXTRICATING yourself from a lie is embarrassing. However, being **EXTRICATED** from an automobile crash can be a matter of life or death. Fortunately, emergency workers have a number of tools specially designed to help **EXTRICATE** injured people from car wrecks and small spaces. These cutters, spreaders, and rams are collectively called "Jaws of Life." Since becoming available to first responders in the 1970s, the "Jaws of Life" have saved countless lives all over the world.

40 | EXEMPLARY

ADJECTIVE—Standing OUT from the norm; outstanding; worthy of imitation

Have you ever been praised for writing an **EXEMPLARY** report, giving an **EXEMPLARY** answer, or designing an **EXEMPLARY** project? If so, you should be proud of yourself. **EXEMPLARY** means to be outstanding and, thus, worthy of imitation. Recording artists and actors are recognized for their **EXEMPLARY** performances by receiving a VMA Moonman, a Grammy, or an Oscar. Scientists and writers are honored for their **EXEMPLARY** work by receiving a Nobel Prize.

41 | ENUMERATE

VERB—To count OUT; to list; to tick off the reasons for

Thomas Jefferson, the author of the Declaration of Independence, felt compelled to **ENUMERATE** the reasons for seeking independence from the crown. In the Declaration of Independence, Jefferson **ENUMERATED** reasons why the colonies declared their independence from Great Britain. The chief concern for Jefferson was the idea of freedom. Jefferson believed that each man living in the colonies should be free from the British King to pursue life, liberty, and happiness.

42 | ELUSIVE
ADJECTIVE—OUT of reach and therefore difficult to catch, define, or describe

The legend of King Arthur and the Knights of the Round Table centers on the search for the **ELUSIVE** Holy Grail. The Holy Grail was the cup used by Christ at the Last Supper and is said to give eternal life. Many of Arthur's knights set out to recover the **ELUSIVE** cup, but most were injured in the pursuit. The legend states that three knights successfully found the Holy Grail and returned it to heaven. Of the three knights, only one returned to tell their tale to King Arthur.

43 | EXORBITANT
ADJECTIVE—Literally OUT of orbit and therefore unreasonably expensive

Serious competition in the NFL occurs both on and off the field. Football stadiums are being rebuilt, each one more lavish than the last. Cowboys Stadium is proof that not only are things bigger in Texas, they are also more **EXORBITANT**! The stadium features 300 luxury suites costing between $100,000 and $500,000 a year with a 20-year lease. Although this may seem pretentious to average fans, the suites provide "the ultimate football experience" by featuring limestone floors, private restrooms, and a special parking lot. The reserved parking is a **COVETED** (Word 119) feature. Parking is limited at Cowboys Stadium. As a result, regular football fans will pay $75 for parking, a price many are calling **EXORBITANT**.

B. *RE*: THE MIGHTY PREFIX *RE* TELLS YOU THAT THINGS ARE COMING BACK AGAIN AND AGAIN

The prefix *RE* means BACK or AGAIN. You are familiar with it in everyday words such as REPEAT, REWIND, and REVERSE. Here are 10 frequently tested words that begin with the prefix *RE*:

44 | REDUNDANT

ADJECTIVE—Needlessly repetitive; saying things AGAIN and AGAIN

PRO TIP

On the standardized tests, the word **REDUNDANCY** usually refers to the duplication or repetition of equipment needed to provide a backup in case the primary systems fail. For example, scuba equipment includes a **REDUNDANT** regulator in case there is a problem with the main air regulator. This **REDUNDANCY** is an important safety precaution.

Political candidates use something called a "stump speech," which is a standard speech given by politicians at campaign events. In the age of the 24 hour news cycle and internet gifs, it is easy to see how **REDUNDANT** these speeches are. With the exception of replacing the name of a town, state, or event location, the "stump speech" is virtually the same speech given over and over again. The **REDUNDANCY** of a campaign message was made clear when Marco Rubio was called out for repeating himself endlessly during a 2016 Republican primary debate. His rivals and some **PUNDITS** (Word 206) **DERIDED** (Word 61) Rubio for only knowing his campaign talking points and being unable to give an answer that was off-script.

45 | REPUDIATE, RECANT, RENOUNCE

VERB—To take BACK; to reject; to disavow

"Martin, do you or do you not **REPUDIATE** these books and the falsehoods they contain?" The place was the Diet of Worms. The time was April 1521. The question posed by the papal legate Johann Eck required an answer. For Martin Luther, the moment of truth had finally arrived. How would Luther respond?

Luther refused to **REPUDIATE** his words, defiantly declaring, "I cannot, I will not **RECANT** these words. For to do so is to go against conscience. Here I stand!" Luther's courageous refusal to **RENOUNCE** his beliefs helped spark the Protestant Reformation.

46 | RELINQUISH
VERB—To surrender or give back (or return) a possession, right, or privilege

The Arab Spring is the name given to the revolutionary wave of demonstrations that began all over the Arab world in December 2010. In January 2011 in Egypt, after 18 days of angry mass protests, President Hosni Mubarak, the longest serving ruler in modern times (30 years), was forced to **RELINQUISH** his position. Power was transferred to the Supreme Council of the Armed Forces (SCAF), and Mubarak was tried and sentenced to life in prison for ordering the killing of peaceful demonstrators. In June 2012, after the first presidential election with more than one candidate since 2005, SCAF, in turn, **RELINQUISHED** its power to the newly-elected president, Mohammed Morsi. Since 2012, Egypt has continued to experience political turmoil. Morsi was removed from power and ultimately sent to prison.

47 | RESILIENT
ADJECTIVE—Bouncing BACK from adversity or misfortune; recovering quickly

RESILIENCE
NOUN—The ability to recover from adversity

The football player was devastated when he injured himself during the first week of football training camp. He was especially upset because he had spent the entire summer training and preparing for the season. The **RESILIENT** athlete followed the advice of his doctors and the team trainers. For six weeks he rehabbed his knee and stood on the sidelines, cheering on his teammates during some of the most exciting games of the season. His hard work and **RESILIENCE** were rewarded when he returned to the line-up and sacked the quarterback on the second play of the game.

48 | REAFFIRM
VERB—To assert AGAIN; to confirm; to state positively

Given at the height of the Cold War, John F. Kennedy's 1961 Inaugural Address **REAFFIRMED** his commitment to freedom when he pledged that America would "pay any price, bear any burden, meet any hardship, support any friend, oppose any foe to assure the survival and success of liberty." Given at the height of the Civil Rights Movement, Dr. King's "I Have A Dream" speech **REAFFIRMED** King's faith in the American dream: "I have a dream that my four little children will one day live in a nation where they will be judged not by the color of their skin but by the content of their character."

49 | RETICENT
ADJECTIVE—Holding BACK one's thoughts, feelings and personal affairs; restrained or reserved

On July 20, 1969, the first man to step onto the surface of the moon, astronaut Neil Armstrong, issued some of the most memorable **APHORISMS** (DH Advanced) of the 20th century: "Houston: Tranquility Base here. The *Eagle* has landed." and "That's one small step for [a] man, one giant leap for mankind." However, he was also known for his **RETICENCE**. Even though he was **REVERED** (DH Essential) as a hero and was awarded the Presidential Medal of Freedom for his work, he refused to give interviews, sign autographs, or make public appearances.

50 | REBUFF
VERB—To repel or drive BACK; to bluntly reject

In the movie *Superman Returns*, Lois Lane **REBUFFS** Superman when she writes an article entitled, "Why the World Doesn't Need Superman." In the movie *Clueless*, Cher claims that Mr. Hall "brutally **REBUFFED**" her plea that he raise her debate grade. In her song "Your Love Is My Drug," Ke$ha remains **RECALCITRANT** (Word 114) as she **REBUFFS** all advice from her friends and family about breaking up with her boyfriend. She says she "won't listen to any advice," even though "momma's telling me I should think twice."

51 | RENOVATE

VERB—To make new AGAIN; to restore by repairing and remodeling

NOV is a Latin root meaning "new." **RENOVATE** thus means to make new again. Hurricane Katrina caused extensive damage in New Orleans and Biloxi, Mississippi. Business and community leaders in both cities vowed to undertake extensive **RENOVATION** projects to restore damaged neighborhoods and revive tourism. For example, in 2007, actor Brad Pitt commissioned 13 architecture firms to submit designs for homes to help **RENOVATE** New Orleans' **IMPOVERISHED** (DH Advanced) Lower Ninth Ward. The project, called *Make It Right*, calls for building 150 affordable, environmentally-sound homes. By June 2016, they had completed 109 of the houses.

52 | REJUVENATE

VERB—To make young AGAIN; to restore youthful vigor and appearance

PRO TIP

The word **REJUVENATE** is formed by combining the prefix *RE* meaning "again" and the Latin root *juvenis* meaning "young." So **REJUVENATE** literally means to be young again.

REJUVENATE is an enticing word. Everyone wants to look and feel young. Health spas promise to **REJUVENATE** exhausted muscles, shampoos promise to **REJUVENATE** tired hair, and herbal medicines promise to **REJUVENATE** worn-out immune systems. However, what people need most to look their best is plenty of water and good sleeping habits!

53 | RESURGENT

ADJECTIVE—Rising AGAIN; sweeping or surging BACK

Apple Computer was founded on April 1, 1976. After great initial success, the company suffered crippling financial losses. However, Apple proved to be **RESILIENT** (Word 47) starting in 1998 with the release of the iMac computer which featured a unique design and new technology. Over the following years, the **RESURGENT** company introduced a series of **INNOVATIVE** (Word 164) and popular products that included the iPhone, the iPad, and the Apple Watch. With its commitment to **INNOVATION** and sleek design, Apple has risen to be one of the most profitable technology companies in the world.

54 | REPUGNANT

ADJECTIVE—Offensive to the mind or senses; causing distaste or aversion; abhorrent

What do a **RANCID** (DH Essential) smell, cheating on an exam, and cannibalism have in common? They are all **REPUGNANT** to us, either physically or morally. Things that some people may find **REPUGNANT** are other people's political views, the use of animals in scientific experiments, and the eating of meat. Many consider the Confederate flag a **REPUGNANT** symbol of slavery.

KNOW YOUR ROOTS

LATIN ROOT:			
PUGN, PUG	fighting (from *pugnus*, a fist)	**PUGNACIOUS**	disposed to fight, quarrelsome, combative
		PUGILIST	a boxer, one who fights with his fists
		REPUGNANCE	fighting back, extreme dislike, aversion, disgust, antipathy
		IMPUGN	to fight against, attack, challenge the motives of

C. *DE*: THE MIGHTY PREFIX *DE* TELLS YOU THAT THINGS ARE HEADED DOWN, DOWN, DOWN

The prefix *DE* means DOWN. You are familiar with *DE* in such everyday words as DEMOLISH, DECLINE, and DEPRESS. Here are eight frequently tested words that begin with the prefix *DE*:

55 | DELETERIOUS

ADJECTIVE—Going DOWN in the sense of having a harmful effect; injurious

What do you think is the fastest growing cause of disease and death in America? The surprising and tragic answer is obesity. As a result of being sedentary and practicing unhealthy eating habits, an **UNPRECEDENTED** (DH Advanced) number of Americans are carrying excess body weight. This excess weight can have a number of **DELETERIOUS** effects, including heart disease, asthma, and diabetes.

A tragic series of recent teen suicides has revealed the **DELETERIOUS** effects of bullying. The **PREVALENCE** (Word 185) of bullying in schools and on the internet has created a **NOXIOUS** (DH Advanced) environment for children and teenagers. In response to the tragedies, the media is shedding light on bullying and its **DELETERIOUS** effects. ABC Family created a campaign called "Delete Digital Drama" in order to help end cyberbullying. The Cartoon Network has also started a campaign called "Stop Bullying: Speak Up", which teaches children what to do when they observe instances of bullying. Lady Gaga has spoken out about her experience with bullying and has vowed to make bullying illegal.

56 | DECRY

VERB—To put DOWN in the sense of openly condemning; to express strong disapproval

During the 1920s, American novelists such as Sinclair Lewis **DECRIED** the era's rampant materialism and conformity. Three decades later, Jack Kerouac and other Beat Generation writers also **DECRIED** sterile middle-class conformity while celebrating spontaneous individualism and creativity through their bohemian lifestyles.

57 | DESPONDENT, MOROSE

*ADJECTIVE—**DOWNCAST** (DH Essential); very dejected; **FORLORN** (DH Essential)*

No character is as **DESPONDENT** as Eeyore from *Winnie the Pooh*. An old gray donkey, Eeyore is characterized by his mopey and pessimistic nature. Just look at how Eeyore feels about his birthday:

"*After all, what are birthdays? Here today and gone tomorrow.***"**

You have to feel bad for **DESPONDENT** Eeyore if he can't even enjoy his own birthday! Luckily, his friends Pooh, Tigger, and Piglet help to **ALLEVIATE** (Word 94) his **MOROSE** mood.

During their 19 years together, Mumtaz Mahal gave Emperor Shah Jahan 14 children. When she suddenly died during childbirth, Shah Jahan was grief-stricken. The now **MOROSE** emperor canceled all appointments and refused to eat or drink for eight days. One historian recorded that when Mumtaz Mahal died, the emperor was in danger of dying himself. When he finally recovered, Shah Jahan built the Taj Mahal as a mausoleum for his beloved wife.

58 | DENOUNCE

VERB—To put DOWN in the sense of a making a formal accusation; to speak against

The pages of history contain a number of inspiring examples of brave individuals who **DENOUNCED** corruption, tyranny, and moral abuses. Voltaire **DENOUNCED** the Old Regime in France, William Lloyd Garrison **DENOUNCED** slavery, Rachel Carson **DENOUNCED** the use of chemical pesticides, and Nelson Mandela **DENOUNCED** apartheid.

59 | DEMISE

NOUN—Sent DOWN in the sense of ending in death; the cessation of existence or activity

What do the dinosaurs and the Whig Party have in common? Each met with a sudden and unexpected **DEMISE**. Paleontologists now believe that a giant asteroid struck the earth about 65 million years ago, causing the **DEMISE** of the dinosaurs and many other plants and animals. Historians point out that the Kansas–Nebraska Act of 1854 brought about the final **DEMISE** of the Whig Party while, at the same time, sparking the rise of the Republican Party. Note that the word **DEMISE** is formed by combining the prefix *DE* meaning "down" with the Latin root *MIS* meaning "to send" (see KNOW YOUR ROOTS p. 79). So **DEMISE** literally means "to send down."

60 | DEBUNK

VERB—To put DOWN by exposing false and exaggerated claims

The longest running reality show on the Syfy Network is about a pair of plumbers turned paranormal investigators. *Ghost Hunters* follows the cases of The Atlantic Paranormal Society, or TAPS. The paranormal investigators, currently led by Jason Hawes, often **DEBUNK** cases of supposed hauntings by rationalizing "ghostly" activity with scientific explanations. Equipment, such as digital cameras, EMF meters, and night vision, is utilized in an effort to determine whether or not a location is haunted. Critics and paranormal **SKEPTICS** (DH Essential) complain that the show is staged and the equipment is not employed properly. The Skeptical Analysis of the Paranormal Society, or SAPS, seeks to **DEBUNK** segments of the show by pointing out inconsistencies in the editing or offering logical explanations for extrasensory experiences.

61 | DERIDE, DERISION

VERB—To put DOWN with contemptuous jeering; to ridicule or laugh at

DERISIVE

ADJECTIVE—Characterized by or expressing contempt; mocking

DERISION

NOUN—The act of mockery; ridicule

The long-running animated sitcom *South Park* is famous for its **DERISIVE** approach to all aspects of society, from the government to religions to celebrities like Tom Cruise, Kanye West, and the *Jersey Shore* cast. The **ICONOCLASTIC** (Word 108) show's creators, Trey Parker and Matt Stone, refuse to be **DEFERENTIAL** (Word 27) to any subject, and they call themselves "equal opportunity offenders." No subject is sacred enough to escape being **SATIRIZED** (Word 8) on the **IRREVERENT** (Word 68) comedy. *South Park's* **DERISIVE** tone is set through this **FACETIOUS** (DH Advanced) disclaimer that airs before each episode: "All characters and events in this show—even those based on real people—are entirely fictional. All celebrity voices are impersonated… poorly. The following program contains coarse language and due to its content should not be viewed by anyone."

DERISION is not limited to television shows. New artistic styles have often been **DERIDED** by both the public and critics. For example, Edouard Manet's painting "Luncheon on the Grass" provoked a storm of scorn and **DERISION**. Hostile critics were **DERISIVE**, calling Manet an "apostle of the ugly and repulsive."

62 | DEVOID, BEREFT

ADJECTIVE—DOWN in the sense of being empty; completely lacking in substance or quality; vacant

What is the worst movie you have ever seen? Why did you select this movie? You probably chose the movie because it was **DEVOID** of humor, plot, and decent acting. Here is a list of movies that were panned by critics for being **BEREFT** of all redeeming value: *The Ridiculous 6, Pixels, Saving Christmas,* and *Cabin Fever.*

D. *IM, IN* AND *IR*: THESE MIGHTY LATIN PREFIXES ALL TELL YOU NO OR NOT

The prefixes *IM, IN, IR,* and *IL* are actually different forms of the same prefix: *IN*, which means NO or NOT. You are familiar with this prefix in everyday words such as INCOMPETENT, IMMATURE, IRREPLACEABLE, and ILLEGAL. See page 43 for five other prefixes that also exist in different forms. Here are seven words that begin with variations of the prefix *IN*.

63 | IMPECCABLE

ADJECTIVE—Having NO flaws; perfect

Look closely at the word **IMPECCABLE**. The prefix IM means "no," and the Latin verb *peccare* means "to sin." So the word **IMPECCABLE** literally means to have no sin and, thus, to be flawless or perfect.

Do you help an older person load groceries into their car and say "yes, sir" and "yes, ma'am" when speaking to adults? If so, you are demonstrating **IMPECCABLE** manners. Do you complete your homework assignments in advance and study for all your tests? If so, you are demonstrating **IMPECCABLE** judgment. Whether manners or judgment, **IMPECCABLE** always means flawless. You can also show **IMPECCABLE** taste and dress **IMPECCABLY**.

64 | IMPLACABLE

*ADJECTIVE—NOT capable of being **PLACATED** (DH Advanced) or appeased*

In his quest to fight for "truth, justice, and the American way," Superman must defeat Lex Luthor and other **IMPLACABLE** foes. Superman is not alone in his struggle against **IMPLACABLE** villains. Spider-Man must defeat the Green Goblin, and Batman's most **IMPLACABLE** enemy is the Joker.

In *Things Fall Apart*, Okonkwo is the **IMPLACABLE** leader of his clan. His drive to succeed leaves him dissatisfied and disappointed with those around him. When the missionaries are unable to convince Okonkwo they only want to help his tribe, it sets off a series of events that do not end well for Okonkwo.

65 | INEXORABLE

ADJECTIVE—NOT capable of being stopped; relentless; inevitable

Although it was a luxury liner, the Titanic did not have the advanced warning systems that modern ships have today. The Titanic did have six lookout guards who stood in the crow's nest and kept a **VIGILANT** (DH Essential) lookout for passing icebergs that could endanger the ship. At 11:40 p.m. on April 15, 1912, Frederick Fleet suddenly spotted an iceberg directly in the ship's path. Fleet urgently informed the bridge, and frantic officers ordered emergency maneuvers. But the ship was traveling too fast. It was on an **INEXORABLE** course to hit the iceberg. The Titanic sank 2 hours and 40 minutes after Fleet's fateful warning.

66 | INCOHERENT

ADJECTIVE—NOT coherent and therefore lacking organization; lacking logical or meaningful connections

One of the most **INCOHERENT** statements ever recorded was uttered in 2007 by a contestant in the Miss Teen USA Pageant. The contestant was told that a recent poll showed that one-fifth of Americans cannot locate the United States on a map. She was asked to explain why. Here is her response in all of its **INCOHERENT** glory:

"*I personally believe that U.S. Americans are unable to do so because, uh, some … people out there in our nation don't have maps and, uh, I believe that our, uh, education like such as in South Africa and, uh, the Iraq, everywhere like such as, and, I believe that they should, our education over HERE in the U.S. should help the U.S., uh, or, uh, should help South Africa and should help the Iraq and the Asian countries, so we will be able to build up our future, for our children.***"*

She later explained that she was flustered by the question and possibly redeemed herself by re-answering the question more coherently on television.

67 | INSURMOUNTABLE

ADJECTIVE—NOT capable of being surmounted or overcome

Beginning in the 1850s, far-seeing American leaders dreamed of building a transcontinental railroad that would bind the nation together. But **SKEPTICS** (DH Essential) argued that while the railroad was a worthy goal, it would face a series of **INSURMOUNTABLE** obstacles that included hostile Plains Indians and the towering, snow-clogged Sierra Nevada mountains. Crews that at times included over 15,000 workers repelled the Indians and blasted tunnels through the mountains. The once **INSURMOUNTABLE** task was completed when Leland Stanford used a silver sledge hammer to drive in the final golden spike on May 10, 1869.

68 | IRREVERENT

ADJECTIVE—Lacking proper respect or seriousness; disrespectful

Even though they go to church every Sunday and pray at the dinner table before many meals, the TV Simpson family members are well-known for their **IRREVERENT** jokes and witticisms. Journalist Mark Pinsky wrote: "*The Simpsons* is consistently **IRREVERENT** toward organized religion's failings and excesses."

Here is one example of an **IRREVERENT** discussion with God.

Homer to God: *"I'm not a bad guy. I work hard and I love my kids. So why should I spend half my Sunday hearing about how I'm going to hell?"*

God: *"Hmm, you've got a point there. You know sometimes even I'd rather be watching football."*

Here is another:

"Dear God, this is Marge Simpson. If you stop this hurricane and save our family, we will be forever grateful and recommend you to all our friends."

69 | IRRESOLUTE

*ADJECTIVE—NOT **RESOLUTE** (DH Advanced); uncertain how to act or proceed; indecisive; **VACILLATING** (DH Advanced)*

Hamlet's father's ghost has assigned Hamlet the task of avenging his father's murder. He knows that his uncle, Claudius, is the murderer, and he has plenty of opportunity, but since he is an **IRRESOLUTE** and **MELANCHOLY** (DH Essential) character given to obsessive brooding, he tends to overanalyze the situation to such a degree that he cannot act. Instead, he **IRRESOLUTELY** thinks, debates, delays, and seeks further proof. Finally, disgusted by his own feeble **IRRESOLUTION**, he observes the Norwegian prince Fortinbras who, with much less cause, is engaged in much more action. He ends this famous soliloquy with the **RESOLUTE** (DH Advanced) declaration: "O, from this time forth, My thoughts be bloody or be nothing worth!"

KNOW YOUR LATIN PREFIXES

In the course of the expansion of the Roman Empire and the relaxation of pronunciation over time, many Latin prefixes that end with a consonant often (but not always) changed their spelling to match the first letter of the roots to which they were attached. This process is called ASSIMILATION, because the root assimilates the prefix and the neighboring sounds become similar. Some other examples of such prefixes, besides *IN-*, are below.

AD- **to, toward**

ACCURATE—done with care, exact

AFFECT—to do something to, to have influence on

ANNOTATE—to add notes to

ADVENTURE—to take a risk, venture toward (*Ad-* does not assimilate here before the v)

COM- **with**

COLLOQUIUM—a speaking together

COMMIT—to send with (*Com-* does not need to change here)

CORRUPT—to break with, spoil

DIS- **apart**

DIFFER—to set apart

DIFFUSE—to spread apart

OB- **against, toward**

OFFER—to bring toward, to present

OCCUR—to run against, to happen

SUB- **under, up from below**

SUFFER—to carry under

SUGGEST—to bring up

SUBTITLE—a subordinate or additional title (*Sub-* does not assimilate here)

E. *CIRCU*: WHAT GOES AROUND COMES AROUND

The prefix *CIRCU* means AROUND. You are familiar with it in everyday words such as CIRCUMFERENCE, CIRCUIT, and CIRCULATION. Here are four frequently tested words that begin with the prefix *CIRCU*:

70 | CIRCUMSPECT

ADJECTIVE—Looking carefully around—thus cautious and careful;
PRUDENT (DH Advanced); discreet

In Homer's *Odyssey*, Penelope cautiously refuses to recognize the much-changed returned Odysseus until he describes their bed, which was built around an olive tree, its trunk functioning as one of the bedposts. No one but her husband would know this fact. Hearing this, the cautious and **CIRCUMSPECT** Penelope is persuaded of the stranger's identity and joyfully welcomes him home.

In Shakespeare's *Hamlet*, Laertes cautions his sister Ophelia to be more **CIRCUMSPECT** in her dealings with Hamlet, a prince whose will is not his own. Laertes says," Then weigh what loss your honor may sustain/ If with too credent ear you list his songs.... Be wary then; best safety lies in fear." Then Polonius, Ophelia and Laertes's father, repeats the same message, ordering her: "Be somewhat scanter of your maiden presence." He hopes that such **CIRCUMSPECTION** will protect her from being dishonored and abandoned.

71 | CIRCUITOUS

ADJECTIVE—CIRCULAR and therefore indirect in language, behavior,
or action, roundabout

In NASCAR, cars race a banked, oval **CIRCUIT** of varying lengths. While NASCAR is hugely popular in the U.S., Formula 1 racing is the most popular auto racing sport globally. Formula 1 takes place on purpose-built tracks and **CIRCUITOUS** street courses. The most famous Formula 1 race is the

Monaco Grand Prix, started in 1929, in which the drivers navigate hairpin turns along a **CIRCUITOUS** route past the Monte Carlo Casino, through a tunnel, alongside luxury yachts, around an outdoor swimming pool before finishing under the enthusiastic gaze of the Royal Family of Monaco.

A **CIRCUIT** is a circular course or journey, like that of the earth around the sun.

72 | CIRCUMVENT

VERB—To circle AROUND and therefore bypass; to avoid by artful maneuvering

During the 1920s, Al Capone and other gangsters built profitable illegal businesses by **CIRCUMVENTING** prohibition laws. Today, illegal businesses continue to **CIRCUMVENT** our laws. For example, drug lords annually smuggle over 100 tons of cocaine and other illegal drugs into the United States.

Sometimes companies **CIRCUMVENT** the law as well. In 2015 Volkswagen was forced to admit that it had designed specific software to **CIRCUMVENT** emissions tests on over 10 million of its cars. By lying to regulators about the emissions of its cars, Volkswagen has had to pay numerous fines and a number of top officials were fired.

73 | CIRCUMSCRIBE

VERB—To draw a line AROUND and therefore to narrowly limit or restrict actions

Juliet (*Romeo and Juliet*) and Janie Crawford (*Their Eyes Were Watching God*) are two famous female literary characters that have to combat the limitations placed on them by others. Although they live in very different times and places, both face restrictions that **CIRCUMSCRIBE** their freedom. Juliet wants to marry Romeo but can't because her family **CIRCUMSCRIBES** her freedom by insisting she marry Count Paris. Janie wants to socialize with a variety of people but can't because her husband **CIRCUMSCRIBES** her freedom by refusing to let her participate in the rich social life that occurs on the front porch of their general store.

F. -OUS: THIS ALL-IMPORTANT SUFFIX MEANS FILLED WITH OR HAVING THE QUALITIES OF

The suffix -OUS means FILLED WITH or HAVING THE QUALITIES OF. You are familiar with it in everyday words such as JOYOUS, COURAGEOUS, and POISONOUS. Here are 13 frequently tested words that end with the suffix -OUS:

74 | MAGNANIMOUS
ADJECTIVE—FILLED WITH generosity and forgiveness; forgoing resentment and revenge

On first glance, **MAGNANIMOUS** looks like a "big" and difficult SAT/ACT word. But looks can be deceiving. Let's use our knowledge of prefixes, roots, and the suffix -OUS to divide and conquer **MAGNANIMOUS**!

The prefix *magna* is easy to recognize. It means "big" as in the word **MAGNIFY**. The root *anim* comes from the Latin *animex* meaning "breath" or soul. An animal is thus a living, breathing thing, and an inanimate object lacks a spirit. And finally, the suffix -OUS means "is filled with" or "having the qualities of." So **MAGNANIMOUS** literally means "filled with a great spirit" and, therefore, generous and forgiving. For example, following Lee's surrender at Appomattox, Grant **MAGNANIMOUSLY** allowed the Confederate officers to keep their sidearms and permitted soldiers to keep personal horses and mules. The Union troops then **MAGNANIMOUSLY** saluted as their defeated foes marched past them.

75 | ERRONEOUS
ADJECTIVE—FILLED WITH errors; wrong

Lil Wayne's **PENCHANT** (Word 194) for tattoos is well known. Fascinated fans have deciphered the meaning of most of Lil Wayne's **MYRIAD** (DH

Advanced) tattoos. However, the three teardrops on his face remain a source of controversy. Many believe that they represent people Lil Wayne has killed. This belief is **ERRONEOUS** and totally unsupported. In his song "Hustler Musik," he clearly states that he has never killed anyone. The three teardrops actually represent family members who have been killed.

76 | MOMENTOUS
ADJECTIVE—FILLED WITH importance; very significant

In 1960, lunch counters throughout the South remained segregated. While moderates urged patience, Joe McNeil and three other black college students disagreed. Calling segregation "evil pure and simple," the four students sat down at a Woolworth's lunch counter in Greensboro, North Carolina, and ordered coffee and apple pie. Although the waitress refused to serve them, the students remained steadfast in their determination to desegregate the dining area. Now known as the Greensboro Four, the students ultimately prevailed. The sit-in movement begun by the Greensboro Four had **MOMENTOUS** consequences. Just four years later, the Civil Rights Act of 1964 **MANDATED** (DH Essential) desegregation in all public places.

77 | MELLIFLUOUS
ADJECTIVE—Smooth and sweet; flowing like honey

Let's divide and conquer the seemingly difficult word, **MELLIFLUOUS**. The Latin roots *mel* meaning "honey" and *fluus* meaning "flow" are the key to understanding **MELLIFLUOUS**. **MELLIFLUOUS** is literally "filled with flowing honey." It almost always is used to describe singers who have sweet-sounding voices. For example, Smokey Robinson, Marvin Gaye, Otis Redding, and Usher are all renowned for their smooth, **MELLIFLUOUS** voices.

78 | ACRIMONIOUS, RANCOROUS
ADJECTIVE—FILLED WITH bitterness; sharpness in words

> **PRO TIP**
>
> **ACUTE**, **ACUITY**, and **EXACERBATE** (DH Advanced) also are related to the Latin *ACER*. **ACUTE** refers to a sharp feeling or sense, such as an acute sense of smell. **ACUITY** means keenness or sharp-sightedness. **EXACERBATE** means to make a problem sharper and thus worse.

What do the words **ACRIMONIOUS**, acid, **ACRID** (Word 22), and **ACERBIC** (Word 22) have in common? All four are derived from the Proto-Indo-European root *ak-*, which means "to be sharp, to rise to a point, to pierce." From that ancient source we get the Latin adjective *acer* (masculine form), *acris* (feminine), *acre* (neuter) meaning sharp, pungent, bitter, eager, and fierce, as well as *acidus*, meaning sharp and sour.

Celebrity divorces often degenerate into **ACRIMONIOUS** contests over money and child custody. While the couples do not throw acid at each other, they often don't hesitate to hurl **RANCOROUS** accusations at their spouses. For example, Denise Richards alleged that Charlie Sheen was "unfaithful and abusive," while Britney Spears called Kevin Federline "the biggest mistake I've ever made." Needless to say, celebrity magazines are only too happy to chronicle all the **ACRIMONIOUS** allegations made by the stars and their lawyers.

79 | COPIOUS
ADJECTIVE—FILLED WITH abundance; plentiful

According to Greek mythology, the cornucopia refers to the horn of a goat that nursed Zeus. The horn had supernatural powers and soon became a symbol of fertility and plenty. In America, the cornucopia has come to be associated with the Thanksgiving harvest. The word **COPIOUS** is derived from the Latin word *copia* meaning "plenty," so **COPIOUS** means filled with plenty and abundant.

In *The Hunger Games*, the arena features a giant horn called the Cornucopia that contains **COPIOUS** amounts of weapons, food, medicine, and other survival equipment. When the Games begin, many of the tributes race to the Cornucopia to fight each other for the best supplies.

80 | ABSTEMIOUS

*ADJECTIVE—FILLED WITH moderation; **TEMPERATE** (Word 201) in eating and drinking*

Abs is a Latin prefix meaning "away or off." For example, absent students are away from school. The Latin word *temetum* means an intoxicating drink. So if you are **ABSTEMIOUS**, you are filled with a desire to stay away from strong drinks. Today, an **ABSTEMIOUS** person can also be moderate or **TEMPERATE** in eating.

81 | MALODOROUS

ADJECTIVE—FILLED WITH an unpleasant odor; foul-smelling

Both stink bugs and skunks can emit a **MALODOROUS** smell. If disturbed, stink bugs emit a liquid whose **MALODOROUS** smell is due to cyanide compounds. Skunks are notorious for their **MALODOROUS** scent glands, which emit a highly offensive smell usually described as a combination of the odors of rotten eggs, garlic, and burnt rubber. The skunk's **MALODOROUS** smell is a defensive weapon that repels predators and can be detected up to a mile away.

82 | HEINOUS, EGREGIOUS

ADJECTIVE—Flagrantly, conspicuously bad; abominable; shockingly evil; monstrous; outrageous

HEINOUS crimes are those that are revolting to the average person, often referred to as Crimes of Moral Turpitude. Perhaps the most **INFAMOUS** (DH Essential) **PERPETRATOR** (DH Essential) of **HEINOUS** acts was Adolf Hitler, the German Nazi implementer of the crimes of the Holocaust.

EGREGIOUS acts are not quite as stunningly monstrous as to be **HEINOUS**, but they are still shockingly bad. Doping in sports is considered one of the most **EGREGIOUS** things an athlete can do, particularly at the Olympics. Athletes can face public warnings, sanctions, and even lifetime bans for the most **EGREGIOUS** cases. They can be sent home in disgrace and stripped of their Olympic medals.

You can use **EGREGIOUS** in a slightly **HYPERBOLIC** (Word 9) way, too, so that you might refer to **EGREGIOUS** grammar errors or **EGREGIOUS** handwriting.

83 | GRATUITOUS

ADJECTIVE—Unwarranted; not called for by the circumstances; unnecessary

PRO TIP

The original meaning of **GRATUITY** was a tip, something extra, not necessary or required but given freely to a waiter, porter, or driver as an extra payment for services rendered. These days a **GRATUITY** is usually expected and is sometimes even added to the bill.

Artistic works, like movies or novels, are sometimes criticized for containing **GRATUITOUS**, or unnecessary, scenes that do not seem essential to the work but seem to be included merely to excite the audience or sell more tickets. For instance, many feel that the violence in Quentin Tarantino's films, such as *Kill Bill*, is over the top and only superficially relevant to the plot. Many horror movies have been criticized for scenes of **GRATUITOUS** sex and nudity.

84 | PRECARIOUS, PERILOUS

ADJECTIVE—Uncertain; characterized by a lack of security or stability

Climbing Mt. Everest, the world's highest mountain, with a peak at 8,850 meters (29,035 feet) above sea level, is **PRECARIOUS** in the best of conditions. Recently, climbers have encountered even more **PERILOUS** conditions with the light snowfall, steep icy slopes, and low oxygen levels, as well as a human "traffic jam" between the last staging camp and the summit, aptly named the "death zone." At the end of the 2012 hiking season, an estimated 150 climbers rushed to take advantage of a short window of good weather, creating even more **PRECARIOUS** conditions and causing the deaths of at least four climbers.

CHAPTER 3 REVIEW

Use the word bank below to help complete the sentences. The answer key is on page 142.

Word Bank:

circumvent	copious	denounced
eccentric	extricated	irreverent
rebuffed	redundant	rebuffed
rejuvenated	precarious	

1. The free climber found herself in a _____ position when she was without footing and blustery winds started blowing.

2. The _____ old woman only wore denim skirts, a purple shirt, and sandals regardless of the weather when walking her cat on a leash around the block.

3. The older her grandfather became, the more _____ his stories. He repeated the same ones over and over again.

4. The _____ bride wore a bright red wedding dress instead of the traditional white.

5. Taking _____ notes in class is one trait of a student with excellent study skills.

6. A week at the beach on her own _____ the working mother of two children. She returned home feeling rested and full of energy.

7. The school _____ the actions of a small group of angry students. In the mind of the administration, no amount of frustration justified book burning.

8. The FBI used a hacker to _____ the security protocols of the terrorist's computer.

9. The trapped fireman had to be _____ from the collapsed building.

10. The popular girls _____ the invitation of the new student for a sleepover.

CHAPTER 4

Sometimes History Repeats Itself

It is **CLICHÉ** (DH Essential) to say that sometimes history repeats itself, but it is true. The words in this chapter span thousands of years of history. As you will see from the examples, empires and leaders often repeat the same mistakes.

85 | SARDONIC, SNIDE

ADJECTIVE—Mocking; derisive; taunting; stinging; SARCASTIC
(DH Essential)

Sir Winston Churchill, Prime Minister of the United Kingdom during World War II, was almost as famous for his **SARDONIC** comments as he was for his steadfast leadership during those **PERILOUS** (Word 84) years.

Bessie Braddock:	Sir, you are a drunk.
Churchill:	Madame, you are ugly. In the morning I shall be sober, and you will still be ugly.
Nancy Astor:	Sir, if you were my husband, I would give you poison.
Churchill:	If I were your husband, I would take it.

In the movie *Avatar*, Dr. Grace Augustine tells Jake, "Just relax and let your mind go blank. That shouldn't be too hard for you." This **SNIDE** remark reveals Grace's initial contempt for Jake.

86 | WRY, DROLL

ADJECTIVE—Dry; humorous with a clever twist and a touch of irony

> **PRO TIP**
>
> A **WRY** sense of humor is different from a **JOCULAR** sense of humor. A **WRY** joke appeals to your intellect and often produces a knowing smile. In contrast, a **JOCULAR** joke appeals to your funny bone and produces a belly laugh.

George Bernard Shaw once sent Winston Churchill some tickets for the first night of one of his plays. Churchill then sent Shaw a **WRY** response, "Cannot come first night. Will come second night if you have one."

Shaw's response was equally **WRY**: "Here are two tickets for the second night. Bring a friend if you have one."

Even though he did not win, *Top Chef* contestant Hugh Acheson's **DROLL** one-liners have helped him become a guest judge on the new TV show *Just Desserts*. He says "I've got youth and **PANACHE** [DH Advanced] and one eyebrow on my side," referring to his famous trademark unibrow.

87 | AUDACIOUS
ADJECTIVE—Fearlessly, often recklessly daring; very bold

General George Washington and Japanese Admiral Isoroku Yamamoto launched **AUDACIOUS** surprise attacks on unsuspecting adversaries. On Christmas Day 1776, Washington ordered the Colonial Army to cross the Delaware and attack the British and Hessian forces at Trenton. Washington's **AUDACIOUS** plan shocked the British and restored American morale.

On December 7, 1941, Yamamoto ordered the Japanese First Air Fleet to launch a surprise attack on the American Pacific Fleet based at Pearl Harbor. Although Japan's **AUDACIOUS** sneak attack temporarily hampered the U.S. fleet, it aroused the now-unified country to demand revenge.

88 | PRAGMATIC
ADJECTIVE—Practical; sensible; NOT idealistic or romantic

In 1933, Franklin D. Roosevelt was a newly-elected president in a country facing the worst economic crisis in its history. For the sake of his country, Roosevelt **PRAGMATICALLY** chose to replace traditional laissez-faire economic policies with "bold, persistent experimentation." FDR **PRAGMATICALLY** explained, "It is common sense to take a method and try it; if it fails, admit it frankly and try another. But above all, try something."

89 | EVOCATION
NOUN—An imaginative re-creation of something; a calling forth
EVOKE
VERB—To call or to summon something, especially from the past

The pyramids of Giza and treasures of King Tut are powerful **EVOCATIONS** of Ancient Egypt. The Great Sphinx **EVOKES** the strength of an incredible civilization, and the jewels of King Tut's tomb **EVOKE** the **OPULENCE** (DH Essential) of the former kingdom.

KNOW YOUR ROOTS		
LATIN ROOT: **VOC,** **VOK** call	**VOCAL**	related to the voice, speaking
	VOCATION	your calling, your profession, often used for a religious career
	AVOCATION	a second calling, a hobby
	EVOKE	to call forth, especially from the past
	REVOKE	to call back, to rescind, to repeal
	INVOKE	to call upon. **EPIC** (Word 11) poems often begin with an Invocation of the Muse, or goddess of artistic inspiration.
	PROVOKE	to call forth (see Word 102)
	CONVOCATION	a calling together, a gathering
	VOCIFEROUS	making an outcry, clamorous
	EQUIVOCATE	to use **AMBIGUOUS** (Word 176) expressions, to mislead
	IRREVOCABLE	incapable of being recalled or altered

90 | AFFABLE, GENIAL, GREGARIOUS

ADJECTIVE—Agreeable; marked by a pleasing personality; warm and friendly; AMIABLE (DH Essential)

President Reagan was renowned for his **AFFABLE** grace and **GENIAL** good humor. On March 6, 1981, a deranged gunman shot the President as he was leaving a Washington hotel. The injured but always **GREGARIOUS** President looked up at his doctors and nurses and said, "I hope you're all Republicans." The first words the President uttered upon regaining consciousness were to a nurse who happened to be holding his hand. "Does Nancy know about us?" the President joked.

KNOW YOUR ROOTS	
LATIN ROOT: ***AMI*** | friend	The English word **AMIABLE** contains the Latin root *ami* meaning friend. You may have heard this root in the French word *ami* and the Spanish word *amigo*.
AMITY	friendship, harmony
AMICABLE	peaceable, harmonious

91 | AUSTERE

ADJECTIVE—Having no adornment or ornamentation; bare; not ORNATE (DH Advanced)

AUSTERITY

NOUN—Great self-denial, economy, discipline; lack of adornment

Ancient Greek architects often used Doric columns to construct temples. For example, the Parthenon's **AUSTERE** columns conveyed strength and simplicity because they lacked ornamentation.

Although modern Greeks admire the **AUSTERE** columns built by their ancestors, they vigorously oppose new **AUSTERITY** measures that raise taxes and cut social welfare programs. These **AUSTERITY** measures provoked massive protests.

92 | ALTRUISM

NOUN—Unselfish concern for the welfare of others

The term was originally **COINED** (DH Advanced) in the 19th century by the sociologist and philosopher of science Auguste Comte. Comte referred to **ALTRUISM** as being the moral obligation of individuals to serve other people and to place others' interests above their own.

Mahatma Gandhi, Martin Luther King, Jr., and Mother Teresa are all people who exemplify **ALTRUISM** through their belief in the basic rights of all people regardless of race, creed, or social standing, and through their service and sacrifices for others.

93 | AUSPICIOUS, PROPITIOUS
ADJECTIVE—Very favorable

How long would you wait to marry your true love? The Mogul princes of India were required to wait until the emperor's astrologers felt that all of the planetary signs were **AUSPICIOUS**. For example, they required Crown Prince Shah Jahan and Mumtaz Mahal to postpone their wedding date for five years. During that time, the lovers were not allowed to see one another. The long-awaited wedding finally took place when all of the astrological signs were **AUSPICIOUS**. The signs must have indeed been **PROPITIOUS** because the royal couple enjoyed 19 years of marital joy and happiness.

94 | MITIGATE, MOLLIFY, ALLEVIATE
VERB—To relieve; to lessen; to ease

Did you know that almost half of all Americans take at least one prescription pill every day? Americans use pills to **ALLEVIATE** the symptoms of everything from migraine headaches to acid indigestion.

Stephen Douglas believed that the doctrine of popular sovereignty would **MITIGATE**, or lessen, the public's passions against the extension of slavery into the territories. But Douglas badly misjudged the public mood in the North. Instead of **MOLLIFYING** the public, popular sovereignty inflamed passions and helped propel the nation toward the Civil War.

95 | FORTITUDE

NOUN—Strength of mind that allows one to endure pain or adversity with courage

William Lloyd Garrison and Rosa Parks demonstrated great personal **FORTITUDE**. While most Americans accepted slavery, Garrison boldly demanded the immediate and unconditional emancipation of all slaves. Although initially ignored, Garrison persevered and lived to see President Lincoln issue the Emancipation Proclamation. Rosa Parks also illustrates the principle that **FORTITUDE** is needed to achieve difficult goals. While most Americans accepted segregation, Rosa refused a bus driver's order to give up her seat to a white passenger. Her historic action helped **GALVANIZE** (DH Advanced) the civil rights movement.

96 | POLARIZE

VERB—To create disunity or dissension; to break up into opposing factions or groups; to be divisive

Americans have a long and distinguished record of settling differences by reaching a compromise. However, some issues are so divisive and **POLARIZING** that a compromise is impossible. Before the Civil War, the issue of slavery **POLARIZED** Americans into two groups: those who defended the South's "peculiar institution" and those who demanded that slavery be abolished. As Lincoln eloquently noted: "A house divided against itself cannot stand. I believe this government cannot endure permanently half slave and half free."

97 | THWART, STYMIE

VERB—To stop; to frustrate; to prevent

At the Paris Peace Conference at the end of World War I, which concluded in the Treaty of Versailles, most of President Woodrow Wilson's proposals for a "Just Peace" were **THWARTED** by the other world leaders, who were more interested in retribution. They did approve his plan for a League of Nations, which he hoped would be able to prevent future wars. When Wilson presented the treaty to the U.S. Senate, there was much opposition. The treaty went down to defeat, Wilson's efforts were again **STYMIED**, and the weak League of Nations, lacking the participation of the world's newest superpower, never achieved its goals.

98 | INTREPID, UNDAUNTED
ADJECTIVE—Courageous; ***RESOLUTE*** *(DH Advanced); fearless*

The American aviator Charles Lindbergh was also **UNDAUNTED** by a seemingly impossible task. Despite several attempts, no pilot had successfully flown across the Atlantic. In 1927, the **INTREPID** Lindbergh electrified the world by flying his single-engine plane, the *Spirit of St. Louis*, from New York to Paris in a grueling 33-hour and 39-minute flight.

99 | ITINERANT
ADJECTIVE—Migrating from place to place; NOT ***SEDENTARY*** *(DH Advanced)*

During the Great Awakening, George Whitefield and other **ITINERANT** ministers touring the Colonies preached their message of human helplessness and divine power. Today, many movie stars also live **ITINERANT** lives. For example, during the last six years, Angelina Jolie and Brad Pitt have lived in 15 homes all over the world, including Paris, Prague, Los Angeles, New Orleans, Berlin, Namibia, India, and New York City. Jolie enjoys her **ITINERANT** lifestyle and says that it is important to experience a variety of cultures.

100 | IMPETUS
NOUN—A stimulus or encouragement that results in increased activity

After the Revolutionary War, life in the colonies was still challenging. Farmers in Massachusetts protested in an armed uprising against tax collectors. Although it was a failure, Shays' Rebellion in 1786 alarmed key American colonial leaders, thus providing the **IMPETUS** for calling a convention to revise and strengthen the Articles of Confederation.

101 | EQUANIMITY

NOUN—Calmness; composure; even-temperedness; poise

George Washington, the great Father of America, was known for his **EQUANIMITY**. He maintained composure no matter what happened around him. Faced with the dangers of battle during the Revolutionary War, Washington remained even-tempered and unflappable. His ability to maintain composure in the heat of battle encouraged his troops to follow and respect him, even during the most devastating times in the Revolution. His **EQUANIMITY** made him an indispensable leader in the early years of the fledgling nation.

102 | PROVOCATIVE

ADJECTIVE—Provoking discussion; stimulating controversy; arousing a reaction

Prior to World War I, young women aspired to seem modest and maidenly. But that changed during the Roaring Twenties. Once modest maidens now **PROVOCATIVELY** proclaimed their new freedom by becoming "flappers." Flappers shocked their elders by dancing the Charleston and wearing one-piece bathing suits. Dismayed by this **PROVOCATIVE** clothing, officials at some beaches insisted on measuring the length of the bathing suits to make sure that they did not reveal too much of the women's legs. In today's world, this notion of **PROVOCATIVE** would seem **ARCHAIC** (Word 144)!

103 | FORTUITOUS

ADJECTIVE—Of accidental but fortunate occurrence; having unexpected good fortune

In the fall of 1862, the South appeared to be on the verge of victory in the Civil War. Following a brilliant triumph at the Second Battle of Bull

Run, General Robert E. Lee boldly invaded Maryland. In war, however, decisive battles are often determined as much by **FORTUITOUS** accident as by carefully planned strategy. As Lee's army steadily advanced, a Union corporal discovered a bulky envelope lying in the grass near a shade tree. Curious, he picked it up and discovered three cigars wrapped in a piece of paper containing Lee's secret battle plans. This **FORTUITOUS** discovery played a key role in enabling the Union forces to win a pivotal victory at the Battle of Antietam.

104 | RHETORICIAN

NOUN—An eloquent writer or speaker

RHETORIC

NOUN—The art of speaking and writing

Frederick Douglass, Franklin Roosevelt, Martin Luther King Jr., John F. Kennedy, and Ronald Reagan were all charismatic leaders and superb **RHETORICIANS** whose eloquent speeches inspired millions of people. For example, in his inaugural address, President Kennedy challenged Americans by proclaiming, "And so, my fellow Americans: ask not what your country can do for you—ask what you can do for your country."

105 | HEDONIST

NOUN—A person who believes that pleasure is the chief goal of life

In Ancient Greece, the **HEDONISTS** urged their followers to "eat, drink, and be merry, for tomorrow we die." Epicurus is the Greek philosopher most closely associated with the **HEDONISTIC** principle of pursuing pleasure. Today most people believe that a **HEDONISTIC** person lives an extravagant life of excess. Epicurus, in his teachings, warned against living a life of overindulgence. He believed that any extreme pursuit would ultimately end in pain.

106 | ASCETIC

NOUN—A person who gives up material comforts and leads a life of self-denial, especially as an act of religious devotion

At the age of 29, Prince Siddhartha Gautama left the luxuries of his father's palace and, for the next six years, adopted an extreme **ASCETIC** life. For days at a time, he ate only a single grain of rice. His stomach became so empty that, by poking a finger into it, he could touch his backbone. Yet, Gautama found only pain, not wisdom. He decided to give up extreme **ASCETICISM** and seek wisdom in other ways. Gautama was successful and soon became known as Buddha, a title meaning "the Enlightened One."

107 | RACONTEUR

NOUN—A person who excels in telling ANECDOTES (DH Advanced)

Herodotus was an ancient Greek historian who was a renowned **RACONTEUR**. Many of the **ANECDOTES** (DH Advanced) in the movie *300* are taken from his famous history of the Persian Wars. For example, Herodotus recounts how a Persian officer tried to intimidate the Spartans by declaring, "A thousand nations of the Persian Empire descend upon you. Our arrows will blot out the sun." **UNDAUNTED** (Word 98), the Spartan warrior Stelios retorted, "Then we will fight in the shade."

108 | ICONOCLAST

NOUN—A person who attacks and ridicules cherished figures, ideas, and institutions

Egyptian pharaoh Akhenaton was an **ICONOCLAST** during his reign from 1353 BC to 1336 BC. Akhenaton challenged ancient Egypt's longstanding belief in a large number of gods by rejecting polytheism and insisting that Aten was the universal or only god. This was a radical position at the time. After his death, Egypt returned to its traditional polytheistic practices.

109 | DEMAGOGUE

NOUN—A leader who appeals to the fears, emotions, and prejudices of the populace

Adolf Hitler is often cited as the perfect example of a **DEMAGOGUE**. Hitler rose to power by using impassioned speeches that appealed to the ethnic and nationalistic prejudices of the German people. Hitler exploited, embittered, and misled WWI veterans by blaming their plight on minorities and other convenient scapegoats.

Unfortunately, Americans have not been immune to the impassioned pleas of **DEMAGOGUES**. During the 1950s, Senator Joseph McCarthy falsely alleged that Communist sympathizers had infiltrated the State Department. As McCarthy's **DEMAGOGIC** rhetoric grew bolder, he **DENOUNCED** (DH Advanced) General George Marshall, former Army Chief of Staff and ex-Secretary of State, calling him "part of a conspiracy so immense and an infamy so black as to dwarf any previous venture in the history of man."

110 | ORACLE

NOUN—A person considered to be a source of wise counsel or prophetic opinions

Would you like to know what is going to happen in the future? All you have to do is ask an **ORACLE**. Just as the ancient Greeks asked the Delphic Oracle to predict the future, 2010 World Cup soccer fans watched televised reports featuring the predictions of an octopus named Paul. The eight-legged **ORACLE** became a global sensation when he correctly predicted the winner of eight straight matches. Paul's **PROGNOSTICATIONS** (DH Advanced) attracted **LUCRATIVE** (DH Advanced) offers from people who wanted to know the outcome of elections and the gender of future children.

111 | SYCOPHANT

*NOUN—A person who seeks favor by flattering people of influence; someone who behaves in an **OBSEQUIOUS** (DH Advanced) or **SERVILE** (DH Advanced) manner*

Louis XIV compelled France's great nobles to live at the Versailles Palace. Life at the royal palace transformed arrogant aristocrats into favor-seeking **SYCOPHANTS**. Instead of competing for political power, nobles **SQUANDERED** (Word 150) their fortunes jockeying for social prestige. For example, nobles vied for the **COVETED** (Word 119) honor of holding Louis XIV's shirt as he prepared to get dressed.

112 | RENEGADE

NOUN—A disloyal person who betrays his or her cause; a traitor; a deserter

> **PRO TIP**
>
> The words **REPROBATE** (Word 166) and **RENEGADE** (Word 112) are easy to confuse. They sound similar, and both are negative words that describe despicable people. A **REPROBATE** is best remembered as a morally unprincipled and evil person. A **RENEGADE** is best remembered as a traitor and deserter.

In 1777, Benedict Arnold was one of America's most admired Revolutionary War generals. Yet, just three years later, Arnold was defamed as a **RENEGADE** whose name became synonymous with traitor. What happened to cause this amazing change in Arnold's reputation? Despite his bravery at the pivotal battle of Saratoga, Arnold was passed over for promotion while other officers took credit for his accomplishments. Frustrated and bitter, Arnold secretly became a British agent. In 1780, he obtained command of West Point, with plans to surrender it to the British. American forces discovered Arnold's treacherous scheme, and he was forced to flee to London to avoid capture. Today, Arnold's contributions to the colonial cause are forgotten, and he is remembered as our nation's first and foremost **RENEGADE**.

CHAPTER 4 REVIEW

Use the word bank below. The answer key is on page 142.

Word Bank:

affable	austere	demagogue	hedonist
provocative	renegade	thwart	wry

Word: _____

Definition in your own words:

_____

Word: _____

Definition in your own words:

_____

Word: _____

Draw it:

Word: _____

Draw it:

Word: _____

Use the word in a sentence that helps explain what it means.

_____

_____

Word: _____

Use the word in a sentence that helps explain what it means.

_____

_____

Word: _____

Use the word in a sentence that helps explain what it means.

_____

_____

Word: _____

Use the word in a sentence that helps explain what it means.

_____

_____

CHAPTER 5

Art and Literature in Context

The world of art and literature is rich with **EVOCATIVE** (Word 89) imagery and cultivated verbiage.

From Jackson Pollock to Shakespeare, this chapter utilizes art and literature to highlight vocabulary needed for the classroom and standardized tests.

113 | INDIFFERENT

ADJECTIVE—Marked by a lack of interest or concern; **NONCHALANT** *(Word 36);* **APATHETIC** *(DH Essential)*

In the classic 80s movie *Ferris Bueller's Day Off*, the economics teacher Ben Stein delivers a sleep-inducing lecture on tariffs and the Great Depression. Stein's bored and **INDIFFERENT** students ignore his monotone lecture. Hoping for some sign of interest, Stein tries asking questions, but his efforts are **FUTILE** (Word 146). Some students are so **APATHETIC** (DH Essential) they fall asleep.

114 | RECALCITRANT, OBSTINATE, OBDURATE

ADJECTIVE—Stubbornly resistant and defiant; **REFRACTORY** *(DH Advanced); disobedient*

In *The Scarlet Letter*, the Reverend Wilson demanded that Hester reveal the identity of the father of her child. But Hester was **RECALCITRANT**. Despite "the heavy weight of a thousand eyes, all fastened upon her," Hester **OBSTINATELY** refused to name the father, defiantly declaring, "Never… I will not speak!"

115 | BOON

NOUN—A timely benefit; blessing

BANE

NOUN—A source of harm and ruin

Fifty Cent was shot nine times and lived! Was the shooting a **BANE** or a **BOON** for his career? At first it was a **BANE** because he had to spend weeks in a hospital in excruciating pain. But the shooting turned out to be a **BOON** for his career because it reinforced Fiddy's "street cred" and attracted lots of publicity.

In Shakespeare's *Othello*, the main character, Othello, fires his lieutenant, Cassio, for inappropriate behavior. Desdemona, Othello's wife, comes to plead for Cassio's reinstatement. She argues that she is not asking for a huge favor: "Why, this is not a **BOON**." She continues that he should instead just think of this request as something normal. Unfortunately for Cassio, the villain Iago is **SURREPTITIOUSLY** (Word 175) working to make Othello think that Desdemona and Cassio are having an affair, even though they are not. Othello, therefore, comes to believe that Cassio is the **BANE** of his existence.

116 | IMPASSE

NOUN—A deadlock; stalemate; failure to reach an agreement

In *The Hunger Games*, the Gamemakers change the rules and announce that two tributes from the same district may win the competition together, so District 12 tributes Katniss and Peeta team up to defeat the others. When they are the only remaining tributes, the Gamemakers revoke the previous rule change and say that only one of them can win in the deadly competition. In response, Katniss takes some poisonous berries from her pouch and shares them with Peeta; they intend to eat the berries together rather than fight each other. Katniss and Peeta are at an **IMPASSE** with the Gamemakers. They would rather die together than fight, and the Gamemakers want only one victor. Finally, the Gamemakers are **COERCED** (DH Advanced) into allowing both victors because of Katniss and Peeta's suicide threat. They would rather have two winners than none.

117 | ANACHRONISM

NOUN—The false assignment of an event, person, scene, or language to a time when the event, person, scene, or word did not exist

Northern Renaissance artists often included **ANACHRONISMS** in their paintings. For example, *Last Supper* by the 15th century artist Dirk Bouts shows Christ and his disciples eating in a royal palace in what is today Belgium. While the **ANACHRONISM** in Bouts's painting is deliberate, the **ANACHRONISMS** in modern movies are unplanned blunders. For example, in the Civil War movie *Glory*, a digital watch is clearly visible on the wrist of a boy waving goodbye to the black soldiers of the 54th Massachusetts Regiment. And in the movie *Gladiator*, you can see a gas cylinder in the back of one of the overturned "Roman" chariots!

KNOW YOUR ROOTS		
GREEK ROOT:	**CHRONOLOGY**	the science of recording events by date
CHRONO | time	**CHRONIC**	continuing for a long time
	SYNCHRONIC	happening at the same time
	SYNCHRONICITY	phenomenon of events which coincide in time and appear meaningfully related but have no discoverable causal connection
	SYNCHRONIZE	to cause to go at the same rate or occur at the same time (as a timepiece or a schedule)
	CHRONICLE	a record of events in order of time
	CHRONICLER	an historian, as a chronicler of events

118 | BELIE

VERB—To contradict; to prove false, appearances that are misrepresentative

In *Jane Eyre*, Edward Rochester is the **AUSTERE** (Word 91) master of the Thornfield estate. He has spent most of his life following his passions and traveling the world. He meets Jane and is captivated by her goodness and morality. Despite seeking to be a better man, Rochester **BELIES** his dinner party guests when he disguises himself as a gypsy fortuneteller. As the pretend psychic, Rochester predicts that Jane will be offered the "cup of bliss." This episode has the desired effect as Jane finds herself falling in love with Rochester.

119 | COVET

VERB—To strongly desire; to crave

COVETOUS

ADJECTIVE—Grasping, greedy, eager to obtain something;
AVARICIOUS (DH Advanced)

The Wizard of Oz tells the story of Dorothy, a small-town Kansas girl, who is magically transported to the land of Oz. The **MALEVOLENT** (Word 29) Wicked Witch of the West is **COVETOUS** of Dorothy's ruby slippers. The witch wants them for herself because she believes the magical slippers will make her more powerful. The Wicked Witch of the West **COVETS** the slippers so desperately that she attempts to kill Dorothy using wolves, bees, and flying monkeys.

120 | ALOOF

ADJECTIVE— Reserved or quiet; disinterested
ADVERB—Detached; distant physically or emotionally; standing near but apart

In *The Great Gatsby*, Fitzgerald initially portrays Jay Gatsby as the **ALOOF** host of lavish parties given every week at his **ORNATE** (DH Advanced) mansion. Although he is courted by powerful men and beautiful women, Gatsby chooses to remain distant and **ALOOF**.

In Homer's *Iliad*, many people accused Zeus of "wanting to give victory to the Trojans." But Zeus chose to remain **ALOOF**: "He sat apart in his all-glorious majesty, looking down upon the Trojans, the ships of the Achaeans, the gleam of bronze, and alike upon the slayers and the slain."

121 | TRITE, BANAL, INSIPID
ADJECTIVE—Unoriginal; commonplace; overused; **CLICHÉD**
(DH Essential)

In *The Catcher in the Rye*, Holden Caulfield just can't help seeing most people as "phony"—his favorite word. When he goes to hear Ernie, the jazz piano player, he thinks of the playing as **BANAL**: so lacking in originality that it is almost boring. He sees straight through his headmaster's platitude that "Life is a game," understanding the message to be **TRITE**, unoriginal, and lacking freshness. Many people who read *The Catcher in the Rye* today think of Holden Caulfield's very character as **INSIPID** because he represents a character we have seen all too many times: the moody, disaffected, disgruntled teenager. But back in 1951, when the novel was first published, Salinger's portrait of a young person was considered searingly original.

122 | SAGE
ADJECTIVE—Profoundly wise or prudent

Luke Skywalker is the central character in the original *Star Wars* trilogy. Over the course of the three films, he struggles with his personal identity and the fight against the dark side. Luke is guided by Yoda, the old and wise mentor. Yoda's **SAGE** advice guides Luke throughout his journey to become the Jedi Knight that he was born to be. Yoda famously said to Luke: "Try not. Do. Or do not. There is no try."

123 | AESTHETIC
ADJECTIVE—Relating to the nature of beauty, art, and taste; having a sense of what is beautiful, attractive, or pleasing

AESTHETICALLY
ADVERB—According to **AESTHETICS** *or its principles and manner*

Do you know why the *Mona Lisa* is considered one of the most beautiful paintings of all time? The answer lies in its use of the

Golden Ratio, the naturally occurring ratio of height to width that is most **AESTHETICALLY** pleasing to humans. The *Mona Lisa*'s face is composed entirely of Golden Ratio rectangles and, thus, adds to the overall **AESTHETIC** of the painting. However, the Golden Ratio is not limited to art. Examples can be found in ancient Greek architecture, Egyptian pyramids, biology, and even widescreen televisions!

It is not **AESTHETICALLY** pleasing if a character introduced at the very end solves a novel or play's conflicts. Aristotle criticized Euripides's play *Medea* for having Medea saved at the end by a character not integral to the plot. To his mind, **AESTHETICALLY** this was not a satisfying conclusion.

124 | PARADOX

NOUN—A seemingly contradictory statement that, nonetheless, expresses a truth

One of the most famous literary first lines is that of Charles Dickens's *A Tale of Two Cities*: "It was the best of times, it was the worst of times." How could such a contradiction be true? In the course of the book, this **PARADOXICAL** statement is shown to be valid.

In Mary Shelley's novel *Frankenstein*, the creature encounters many **PARADOXES**. One is the simultaneous positive and negative characteristics of fire. It can warm him, protect him, light his way, and cook his food, but it can also burn and destroy. Similarly, the creature also comes to recognize the **PARADOXICAL** nature of man: driven by conflicting forces of selfishness and **ALTRUISM** (Word 92).

125 | ENIGMATIC, INSCRUTABLE

ADJECTIVE—Mysterious; puzzling; unfathomable; baffling

Dutch painter Vermeer's portrait of a *Girl With a Pearl Earring* is considered one of history's most **ENIGMATIC** paintings. For centuries, art lovers and historians have wondered about her true identity. Because the painting depicts a young woman against a black background and in nondescript clothing, it is impossible to detect any identifying features. The **INSCRUTABLE** painting was the inspiration for the historical fiction novel *A Girl With a Pearl Earring,* which later became a successful movie. Despite over 300 years of investigation and research, the girl's identity remains a mystery.

126 | AUTONOMY

NOUN—Independence; self-governance

AUTONOMOUS

ADJECTIVE—Acting independently, or having the freedom to do so; not controlled by others

Fahrenheit 451, the classic novel by Ray Bradbury, imagines a dystopian society in which a faceless government exerts huge control over its citizens. No books are allowed; instead, citizens watch endless television streams of propaganda from the government. Bradbury's novel suggests that people naturally desire **AUTONOMY** in their own lives. If a faceless government tries to exert **AUTHORITY** (DH Essential) over them, they will tend to be subversive and rebel against that power.

In the movie *Men in Black*, Agent Zed explains that MIB is an **AUTONOMOUS** organization that is "not a part of the system." He goes on to say that MIB is "above the system, over it, beyond it; we are they, we are them, we are the Men in Black." They are serious about their **AUTONOMY**!

127 | NEBULOUS

ADJECTIVE—Vague; cloudy; misty; lacking a fully-developed form

Have you read the Epilogue in *Harry Potter and the Deathly Hallows*? If you found it rather vague, then J.K. Rowling achieved her goal. In an interview, Rowling stated that the Epilogue is deliberately "**NEBULOUS.**" She wanted readers to feel as if they were looking at Platform 9 3/4 through the mist, unable to make out exactly who was there and who was not.

128 | BEREFT

ADJECTIVE—Deprived of or lacking something

Shakespeare's *Hamlet* is filled with characters wrestling with a **MYRIAD** (DH Advanced) of issues, but Ophelia is Shakespeare's most **BEREFT** character. Ophelia, sinking further into her own madness, cannot seem to overcome Hamlet's rejection. Rather than face life without him, she drowns herself.

129 | CALLOUS

ADJECTIVE—Emotionally hardened; insensitive; unfeeling

In the movie *Mean Girls*, the Plastics **CALLOUSLY** mistreat their classmates. They even keep a "Burn Book" filled with **CALLOUS INNUENDOES** (Word 197) and **SARCASTIC** (DH Essential) putdowns.

In F. Scott Fitzgerald's novel *The Great Gatsby*, Tom Buchanan **CALLOUSLY** ruins the lives of four people (Daisy, Gatsby, Myrtle, and George) while recklessly pursuing his own selfish pleasures.

130 | BUCOLIC, RUSTIC, PASTORAL

ADJECTIVE—Characteristic of charming, unspoiled countryside and the simple, rural life

Americans have always been proud of our country's great natural beauty. During the early 19th century, a group of artists known as the Hudson River School specialized in painting the **RUSTIC** beauty of America's unspoiled landscape. Today, many students are attracted to the **PASTORAL** beauty of campuses located in small towns. For example, one writer described Blacksburg, Virginia, the home of Virginia Tech, as "a quaint, off-the-beaten-track, **BUCOLIC** college town nestled in the mountains of southwest Virginia."

131 | ANGUISH

NOUN—Agonizing physical or mental pain; torment

Ancient Greek tragedies are filled with the unhappiness, pain, failure, and loss associated with the human condition. In Sophocles's *Antigone*, King Creon of Thebes refused to give his nephew a proper burial after he was killed in a battle against his own brother. Creon's niece, Antigone, **ANGUISHED** at this breach of protocol, tries to carry out the funeral rites and is walled up in a cave as punishment. Creon remains **OBDURATE** (Word 114) until he hears of the suicides of his wife and his son (Antigone's fiancé) after Antigone hangs herself. Too late and **REMORSEFUL** (DH Advanced), Creon is left to deal with his **ANGUISH** totally alone.

132 | SUPERFICIAL

ADJECTIVE—Shallow; lacking in depth; concerned with surface appearances

Daisy Buchanan, in *The Great Gatsby*, proves to be a **SUPERFICIAL** person who prizes material possessions. For example, she bursts into tears when Gatsby shows her his collection of English dress shirts because she realizes that he has now become seriously wealthy. Tragically, Gatsby discovers that beneath Daisy's **SUPERFICIAL** surface there is only more surface.

KNOW YOUR PREFIXES		
LATIN PREFIX:	**SUPERCILIOUS**	overbearing, proud, haughty
SUPER, over, above,	**SUPERFICIAL**	on the surface, shallow
SUPRA greater in quality	**SUPERLATIVE**	the best, in the highest degree
	SUPERNATURAL	above and beyond all nature
	SUPERSEDE	to take the place of

133 | DISMISSIVE

*ADJECTIVE—Showing overt intentional **INDIFFERENCE** (Word 113) or disregard; rejecting*

Jackson Pollock, the famous American abstract expressionist painter, had to overcome **DISMISSIVE** critics. Bewildered critics ridiculed Pollock, calling him "Jack the Dripper." The rejection of Pollock's signature drip style of painting did not dissuade Pollock from continuing his work. By 1950, he was considered to be the greatest living painter in the United States.

KNOW YOUR ROOTS

LATIN ROOT: ***MITT MISS*** to send		
	EMIT	to send out
	SUBMIT	to send under, yield, resign, surrender
	TRANSMIT	to send across, communicate, convey
	REMIT	to send back, pay money, diminish in intensity
	OMIT	to send by, pass by, neglect, leave out
	ADMIT	to send to, let in, confess, concede
	COMMIT	to send together, entrust, pledge, memorize
	PERMIT	to send through, allow
	DISMISS	to send away, discharge, put out of mind
	REMISS	negligent, lax, careless
	REMITTANCE	a payment sent to pay a bill
	MISSION	a duty one is sent to perform
	MISSILE	something sent through the air
	MISSIVE	a note sent by messenger
	EMISSARY	a messenger sent on a mission

134 | POMPOUS, PRETENTIOUS

ADJECTIVE–Filled with excessive self-importance; OSTENTATIOUS (DH Essential); boastful

Poe's *The Tell-Tale Heart* is the story of a murder told from the perspective of the unnamed narrator. While the **PERPETRATOR** (DH Essential) is clearly mad, he is also incredibly **POMPOUS**. When the police arrive to investigate the source of the screams heard by a neighbor, the murderer invites them in to look around the house. He is so **PRETENTIOUSLY** confident in his ability to commit the perfect murder, that he invites the officers to sit in the very room where the poor old man is buried beneath the floorboards. Ultimately, it is a combination of his self-importance and madness that reveal his crime.

135 | CRYPTIC

ADJECTIVE–Having a hidden or AMBIGUOUS (Word 176) meaning; mysterious

As *Harry Potter and the Chamber of Secrets* opens, Dobby delivers this **CRYPTIC** message to Harry: "Harry Potter must not go back to Hogwarts." But why must Harry stay away from Hogwarts? Since the message is so **CRYPTIC**, we don't know. Later in the same book, a **CRYPTIC** message appears on one of the walls at Hogwarts: "The Chamber of Secrets has been opened. Enemies of the Heir, Beware." Once again, since the message is **CRYPTIC**, we are not sure what it means.

136 | SUBTLE

ADJECTIVE–Difficult to detect; faint; mysterious; likely to elude perception

Iago, the ultimate villain of English literature, is brilliantly **SUBTLE** in the way he manipulates Othello into believing that his wife, Desdemona, has been unfaithful. Iago **SUBTLY** plants suspicion with diversions, suggestions, and **INNUENDOES** (Word 197). This **SUBTLETY** makes Othello more deeply **APPREHENSIVE** (DH Essential), and so Iago's

NEFARIOUS (DH Advanced) plan succeeds in destroying both Othello and Desdemona.

137 | CHARLATAN

NOUN—A fake; fraud; imposter; cheat

PRO TIP

The word **CHARLATAN** often appears in sentence completion questions. A **CHARLATAN** is associated with negative traits. A **CHARLATAN** will try to dupe unwary victims with **SPURIOUS** (DH Advanced) information.

Would you trust the Wizard of Oz, Gilderoy Lockhart (*Harry Potter and the Chamber of Secrets*), or Chaucer's Friar (*The Canterbury Tales*)? I hope not. All three of these men were **CHARLATANS**, imposters who could not be trusted. The Wizard of Oz was a **CHARLATAN** who tried to trick Dorothy and her friends. Gilderoy Lockhart was a **CHARLATAN** who interviewed famous wizards and witches and then took credit for their heroic deeds. The Friar, a member of a medieval begging order, was supposed to beg from the rich and give to the poor. Instead, he spent his time with well-off people, knew all the taverns, and dispensed pardons based solely on the amount of money he was given. It is even suggested that he had an active love life that required him to find husbands for the young women he had made pregnant.

138 | BUFFOON

NOUN—A person who amuses others with odd behavior and jokes; clown; jester; fool

The Fool is one of the most vital character archetypes in literature. On the surface, these **BUFFOONS** could be easily dismissed as having no purpose beyond comic relief. However, the Fool is far more complex. In addition to tricks and jokes, the **BUFFOON** is often used as a means to flesh out other characters' true intentions. Additionally, the jester of a story can be the protagonist's conscience. The **CLICHÉ** (DH Essential) that there is truth in humor is rooted in the role the **BUFFOON** has played in literature over the centuries.

139 | RECLUSE

NOUN—A person who leads a secluded or solitary life

Emily Dickinson is one of America's most **PROLIFIC** (DH Advanced) poets, writing close to 2,000 poems in her lifetime. Emily was also a **RECLUSE**. She lived her entire life in the the same house and almost never left home. She never married and chose to keep most of her writing private. Only about a dozen of Emily's poems were published while she was alive. It was after her death that her sister found a trunk full of her writing. Many of her poems elaborated on her solitary life:

"*I hide myself within my flower,*
That wearing on your breast,
You, unsuspecting, wear me too --
And angels know the rest.

I hide myself within my flower,
That, fading from your vase,
You, unsuspecting, feel for me
*Almost a loneliness.***"**

Emily Dickinson

140 | CLAIRVOYANT

NOUN—A person with the supposed power to see objects and events that cannot be perceived with the five traditional senses

ADJECTIVE—Having the ability to see into the future or beyond the normal senses

Cassandra is Shakespeare's **CLAIRVOYANT** in *Troilus and Cressida*. Because she spoke about future death and disaster, she was ignored and presumed crazy. The truth was that Cassandra had been given the gift of seeing into the future by Apollo, the Greek god. Had her brothers listened to her predictions about the dangers of keeping Helen, then perhaps Troy would not have burned.

141 | PRODIGY

NOUN—A person with great talent; a young genius

Both Wolfgang Mozart and Pablo Picasso were **PRODIGIES** who demonstrated uncanny artistic talent at a young age. Mozart was a child **PRODIGY** who wrote his first symphony at the age of eight and grew into a **PROLIFIC** (DH Advanced) adult who wrote over 600 pieces of music before his death at the age of 35. Like Mozart, Picasso also demonstrated **PRECOCIOUS** (DH Essential) talent, drawing pictures before he could talk. Picasso mastered many styles but is best known as the originator of Cubism.

142 | MISANTHROPE

NOUN—A person who hates or distrusts humankind

PRO TIP

MISANTHROPE combines the Greek prefix *MISO* meaning "hate" with the Greek root *ANTHROPOS* meaning "humankind." Prefixes make a difference in the meaning of words. If we place the Greek prefix *PHILO*, meaning "love," in front of *ANTHROPOS*, we form the word **PHILANTHROPY**, meaning love of humankind. A **PHILANTHROPIST** loves humanity so much that he or she donates time and money to charity.

Ebenezer Scrooge and Alceste are two of the best-known **MISANTHROPES** in literature. Scrooge is the main character in Charles Dickens's 1843 novel, *A Christmas Carol*. He is a cold-hearted, **FRUGAL** (DH Essential) **MISANTHROPE** who despises poor people and Christmas.

Alceste is the main character in Molière's 1666 play, *The Misanthrope*. He is a judgmental **MISANTHROPE**, quick to criticize the flaws in people.

CHAPTER 5 REVIEW

Complete each word box. The answer key is on page 143.

Unoriginal; overused; commonplace:

Word 1: _____

Word 2: _____

Word 3: _____

Characteristic of the charming countryside:

Word 1: _____

Word 2: _____

Word 3: _____

Indifferent:
Definition in your own words: _____

_____

Impasse:
Definition in your own words: _____

_____

Sage:
List 3 synonyms: _____

Bereft:
List 3 synonyms: _____

Anguish:
List 3 synonyms: _____

Pompous:
List 3 synonyms: _____

Buffoon:
Use the word in a sentence that helps explain what it means.

_____

_____

_____

Prodigy:
Use the word in a sentence that helps explain what it means.

_____

_____

_____

CHAPTER 6

Science Can Be Social

Sociology, Physics, and Environmental Biology are just some of the fascinating fields of study filled with rich and diverse words. This chapter puts the vocabulary of science under the microscope.

143 | CONJECTURE
NOUN—An inference based upon guesswork; a supposition

What caused the sudden extinction of dinosaurs? Scientists have offered a number of **CONJECTURES** to explain why the Age of Dinosaurs came to an abrupt end. One popular **CONJECTURE** suggests that a giant meteor struck Mexico's Yucatan Peninsula, causing widespread firestorms, tidal waves, and the severe downpour of acid rain. An alternative **CONJECTURE** suggests that massive volcanic eruptions at the Deccan Flats in India caused climate changes that killed the dinosaurs. While both **CONJECTURES** are **PLAUSIBLE** (DH Essential), scientists still lack a definitive explanation.

144 | OBSOLETE, ARCHAIC, ANTIQUATED
ADJECTIVE—No longer in use; outmoded in design or style

For many years, Kodak was the iconic leader in the photo industry. Many of its products became **ANTIQUATED** and, in the case of camera film, nearly **OBSOLETE**. Kodak's shortsighted business model caused them to be late in entering the successor market—digital photography.

145 | PROTOTYPE
NOUN—An original model; an initial design

What do the Model T and The Bat in *The Dark Knight Rises* have in common? Although very different vehicles, both were originally designed to be **PROTOTYPES**. The Model T, invented by Henry Ford in 1908, served as the **PROTOTYPE** for the world's first affordable, mass-produced automobile. The Bat, created by Lucius Fox at Wayne Enterprises, was a **PROTOTYPE** for a flying tank military vehicle, but it helped Batman save Gotham from Bane and his men.

146 | FUTILE
ADJECTIVE—Completely useless; doomed to failure; in vain

The Deepwater Horizon oil spill released a **COLOSSAL** (DH Essential) flood of crude oil into the Gulf of Mexico. BP engineers made repeated attempts to control or stop the spill. However, all of their initial efforts proved to be **FUTILE**. Although crews worked tirelessly to protect hundreds of miles of beaches, wetlands, and estuaries, local residents worried that these efforts would also prove to be **FUTILE**.

147 | INDIGENOUS, ENDEMIC
ADJECTIVE—Native to an area

AGRICULTURAL (DH Essential) sustainability largely depends on responsible growing practices. For centuries, **CULTIVATING** (DH Essential) **ENDEMIC** farms and gardens has not been as important as making a profit or creating a pleasing **AESTHETIC** (Word 123). Non-**INDIGENOUS** plants such as English ivy are common all over the country. English ivy will climb **INDIGENOUS** trees, choking out the branches and sunlight until the trees eventually die.

KNOW YOUR ROOTS		
GREEK ROOT: **DEM,** **DEMO** the people	**PANDEMIC** (Word 148)	of all the people, prevalent over a whole area
	DEMOCRACY	rule by the people, by the majority
	DEMAGOGUE (Word 109)	a person who tries to stir up the people by appealing to emotion and prejudice in order to achieve selfish ends
	DEMOGRAPHICS (DH Advanced)	the science of vital statistics about populations (births, deaths, marriages, incomes, etc.)
	EPIDEMIC	a rapid spread of a contagious disease or other negative condition

148 | PANDEMIC

NOUN—An epidemic that is geographically widespread and affects a large proportion of the population

In 2015, there was an outbreak of the Zika virus in Brazil. The virus is spread through mosquitos and causes birth defects in pregnant women. The outbreak strongly intensified throughout the start of 2016 with over 1.5 million cases reported in the Americas. If not controlled, the Zika virus has the possibility of becoming a global **PANDEMIC**, affecting billions of people worldwide.

PANDEMIC can also be used as an adjective, meaning **PREVALENT** (Word 185) over a large area.

149 | ADROIT, DEFT, DEXTEROUS

ADJECTIVE—Having or showing great skill; nimble; ADEPT (DH Essential)

PRO TIP

Are you right-handed or left-handed? Right-handed people were once thought to be more **ADROIT** and **DEXTEROUS** than left-handed people. This bias can be seen in the etymology of these two words. The English word **ADROIT** is actually derived from the French word *droit* meaning right, as opposed to left. So if you are **MALADROIT**, you are not skillful. The ancient Romans shared the same positive view of right-handed people. The Latin word *dexter* means right, as opposed to left.

What do 16-year-old Austin Wierschke and action star Chuck Norris have in common? Austin has **DEXTEROUS** hands, and Chuck has **ADROIT** legs. Austin won the U.S. National Texting Championship two years in a row. He beat out 11 other finalists by **DEFTLY** texting blindfolded, texting with his hands behind his back, and by enduring rounds of marathon texting. As everyone knows, Chuck Norris is **ADEPT** (DH Essential) at using a roundhouse kick to escape even the toughest situations. In fact, it is rumored that if someone were **DEFT** enough to harness the energy from a Chuck Norris roundhouse kick, he or she could power the entire country of Australia for 44 minutes.

150 | SQUANDER

VERB—To spend thoughtlessly; to waste

Former Virginia Governor Bob McDonnell and his wife are headed to jail. On January 21, 2014, they were indicted on federal corruption charges for receiving improper gifts and loans from a Virginia businessman. They were convicted on most counts by a federal jury, making McDonnell the first Virginia governor to be convicted of a felony. People in his state were stunned that he **SQUANDERED** his political career and future for gifts of trips and shopping sprees. Not only did Governor McDonnell throw away any chance of holding political office again, but he and his wife will both serve jail time.

KNOW YOUR ROOTS

LATIN ROOT:		
MON | to warn, remind	**ADMONITION**	a warning or reproof, a reminder
	PREMONITION	a warning in advance, **FORESHADOWING** (Word 12) of something evil, foreboding
	MONITOR	a person or a device that reminds or checks (like a study hall monitor, a heart monitor, or an audio monitor for performers on a stage)
	MONUMENT	a sepulchre, memorial, edifice to commemorate something or someone notable, something that reminds (literally)

151 | INCONTROVERTIBLE

ADJECTIVE—Impossible to deny or disprove; demonstrably true

In recent years, the global warming debate has grown increasingly heated (no pun intended), politicized, and **POLARIZED** (Word 96). Al Gore's film, *An Inconvenient Truth*, presented statistics that many people challenge. But it is becoming clear that global warming is an **INCONTROVERTIBLE** fact. What is less clear has been the cause of the climatic changes. Many concede the existence of the trend but claim that the current trend is merely part of a natural meteorological cycle. Others lay the blame on humans' emission of greenhouse gases. According to Richard A. Muller, a former **SKEPTIC** (DH Essential) whose Berkeley Earth Surface Temperature project has persuaded him of human culpability in global warming, the changes are too great to be attributed to urban heating, solar activity, world population, normal fluctuations, or manipulation of data. Only changes in the carbon dioxide curve match the changes in world temperatures. So, the **SKEPTIC** has been persuaded that man is, **INCONTROVERTIBLY**, playing a part in the climate changes we are now experiencing.

152 | CONVOLUTED

ADJECTIVE—Winding, twisting, and, therefore, difficult to understand; intricate

The 2016 presidential election has highlighted the Electoral College. Many Americans falsely believe that we are a democracy, where one person equals one vote. However, our election process is a bit more **CONVOLUTED**. The United States is a democratic republic. Therefore, when individuals vote for president, they are actually voting for a group of people knowns as electors. These electors are part of the Electoral College. It is understandable that so many Americans are frustrated by a complicated process that, at times, does not seem to properly represent the will of the people.

153 | PLACID, SERENE

ADJECTIVE—Calm or quiet; undisturbed by tumult or disorder

Where did Lake **PLACID** get its name? No one is really sure. Some suggest that the lake is so calm and **SERENE** that the original settlers felt totally at peace there. The lake itself acts like a mirror, reflecting the **BUCOLIC** (Word 130) surroundings. At one point, Lake **PLACID**, New York, became a refuge for freed slaves. Later, it hosted the 1932 and 1980 Winter Olympics.

KNOW YOUR ROOTS

LATIN ROOT:		
PLAC | to quiet, soothe, pacify, please	**IMPLACABLE** (Word 64)	unappeasable, inexorable
	PLACATE	to appease or calm someone's anger
	PLACID	calm, quiet
	COMPLACENT	self-satisfied, smug
	COMPLAISANT (DH Advanced)	disposed to please (note French *plaisir*), affable, gracious

154 | VIABLE, FEASIBLE
ADJECTIVE—Capable of being accomplished; possible

Variable oil costs and worries about global warming have prompted a search for **VIABLE** alternatives to fossil fuels. Some of the most **FEASIBLE** alternative energy sources include solar power, wind power, and biofuels. However, currently only around eight percent of energy in the United States comes from renewable sources, meaning that much research is still needed in order to find **VIABLE** alternative energy sources. Companies like BP and GE have invested billions of dollars in research on the most **FEASIBLE** sources of energy.

155 | DISPARITY
NOUN—An inequality; a gap; an imbalance

PRO TIP

DISPARITY contains the Latin root *PAR* meaning "that which is equal." The root still lives in the golfing term *PAR*, which means to be equal to the course. It can also be seen in the word **PARITY**, which means equality in status or value.

The Hunger Games takes place in the nation of Panem, which contains 12 districts controlled by the **DESPOTIC** (DH Advanced) President Snow, who rules the country from the Capitol. There is great **DISPARITY** in Panem between the **AFFLUENT** (DH Advanced) and spoiled citizens of the Capitol and the **IMPECUNIOUS** (DH

Advanced) residents of the districts, who live in very poor conditions and suffer from starvation. The **DISPARITY** is especially evident during the annual Hunger Games, in which the districts are forced to send teenagers to compete in a **MORTAL** (DH Essential) battle for the Capitol's entertainment.

Mumbai (formerly Bombay) is India's financial capital and largest city. The movie *Slumdog Millionaire* features vivid images of the **DISPARITY** between the **AFFLUENT** (DH Advanced) few who live in the city's luxury condominiums and the poverty-stricken masses who live in tiny shacks in the densely-crowded Dharavi slum.

156 | CURTAIL
VERB—To cut short or reduce

The 2010 Gulf Oil Spill created an **UNPRECEDENTED** (DH Advanced) environmental and economic disaster. As a toxic oil slick spread across the Gulf's once **PRISTINE** (DH Advanced) beaches and wetlands, **IRATE** (DH Essential) workers lost jobs while worried tourists **CURTAILED** and even canceled vacation trips to the region. The spill emphasized America's dependence upon gasoline. On average, Americans consume about 386 million gallons of gasoline each day. This huge rate of consumption cannot go on forever. Many **PUNDITS** (Word 206) argue that Americans must **CURTAIL** their fuel consumption by developing renewable sources of energy.

157 | INNOCUOUS
ADJECTIVE—Harmless; unlikely to give offense or to arouse strong feelings or hostility

Many mushrooms are **INNOCUOUS**, but there are some, like the Amanita or Death Cap mushroom, that are poisonous and should not be eaten.

Sometimes a person will say something unkind and then claim that the intent was **INNOCUOUS**, saying, "Oh, they know I'm kidding." Such an assertion may very well be **DISINGENUOUS** (DH Advanced), for the speaker is probably quite aware of the toxic effect of the not-so-**INNOCUOUS** words.

158 | DIATRIBE, TIRADE, HARANGUE

NOUN—A bitter abusive denunciation; a thunderous verbal attack

Coach Carter (*Coach Carter*), Coach Taylor (*Friday Night Lights*), and Coach Boone (*Remember the Titans*) are passionate about building character and teamwork. And, if necessary, all three don't hesitate to deliver a **TIRADE** when a player fails to follow team rules or perform to the best of his ability. For example, Coach Boone demands perfection. In one memorable **DIATRIBE** he insists, "We will be perfect in every aspect of the game. You drop a pass, you run a mile. You miss a blocking assignment, you run a mile. You fumble the football, and I will break my foot off in your John Brown hind parts and then you will run a mile. Perfection. Let's go to work!"

It is debatable as to whether **HARANGUING** others in order to inspire them to different behaviors is an effective strategy. Former Indianapolis Colts coach, Tony Dungy, refused to **RANT** (DH Essential) at his players and achieved great success, including winning the Superbowl.

159 | PARTISAN

NOUN—A supporter of a person, party, or cause; a person with strong and perhaps biased beliefs

Are you pro gun control or pro NRA? Do you support health care reform legislation? How do you feel about illegal immigration? If you have a strong view on these issues, you are a **PARTISAN**. In contrast, **NONPARTISAN** issues enjoy widespread public support. For example, during the Cold War, most Americans supported the policy of containing Soviet expansion.

160 | PROGNOSTICATOR

NOUN—A person who makes predictions based upon current information and data

PRO TIP

In medicine, a doctor will often give a patient his **PROGNOSIS**. A **PROGNOSIS** is a forecast concerning the causes of his disease and outlining the chances of recovery.

Weather forecasters, sports announcers, and financial analysts are all **PROGNOSTICATORS** who use information and data to make predictions and forecasts. It is important to understand the difference between a **PROGNOSTICATOR** and a **CLAIRVOYANT** (Word 140). Although both make predictions, a **PROGNOSTICATOR** uses empirical data that can be collected, seen, and studied. In contrast, a **CLAIRVOYANT** claims to see the future through means beyond the five senses.

161 | DICTATOR

NOUN—A person exercising absolute power, especially a ruler who has absolute, unrestricted control in a government

Kim Jong-un is the Supreme Leader of North Korea. He is an unpredictable **DICTATOR**, regularly in the news for his nuclear missile tests and threats to go to war against South Korea and the United States. He has complete **AUTHORITY** (DH Essential) over his country, controlling information and travel. He is **INFAMOUS** (DH Essential) for his **LAVISH** (DH Essential) lifestyle while a vast majority of his people are on the brink of starvation. Additionally, Kim Jong-un is known for eliminating detractors. Kim executed his uncle and second-in-command for "attempting to overthrow the state by all sorts of intrigues and despicable methods with a wild ambition to grab the supreme power of our party and state."

162 | PATRON, BENEFACTOR *(DH Essential)*

NOUN—A person who makes a gift or bequest

BENEFICIARY

NOUN—The recipient of funds, titles, property, and other benefits

Nicholas Sparks has achieved international fame by writing romance novels such as *The Notebook* and *A Walk to Remember* that are often set in New Bern, North Carolina. Residents of New Bern also know Sparks as a generous **BENEFACTOR** (DH Essential) and **PATRON** who has donated nearly $1 million to build a state-of-the-art track and field facility for New Bern High School. As the **BENEFICIARIES** of this **MUNIFICENCE** (DH Advanced), the New Bern Bears have become one of North Carolina's top track and field teams. Note that both **BENEFACTOR** and **BENEFICIARY** begin with the Latin root *bene*, which means "good." So a **BENEFACTOR** (DH Essential), like Nicholas Sparks, gives good gifts, and a **BENEFICIARY**, like New Bern High School, receives good gifts.

KNOW YOUR ROOTS		
LATIN ROOT:	BENEFIT	to do good, (noun) a good thing
BENE good, well	BENEFICIAL	good, wholesome
	BENEFICENT	doing good
	BENEFACTOR	one who helps another
	BENEVOLENCE	good will towards others
	BENEDICTION	the act of blessing

163 | PROPONENT, ADVOCATE

NOUN—One who argues in support of something; a champion of a cause

Although America has faced a number of challenging social problems, our nation has always produced leaders who were strong **PROPONENTS** of reform. For example, during the 19th century, Jane Addams was an outspoken **PROPONENT** of urban settlement houses. Today, former Vice-President Al Gore is a vigorous **ADVOCATE** of implementing measures that will reduce global warming. One way to remember **PROPONENT** is to note that the prefix *pro* means to be *for* something.

KNOW YOUR ROOTS

LATIN ROOT: **PONE, POSE** to place, set, put		
	EXPOSE	to set forth, to show for all to see
	DEPOSE	to remove from office
	REPOSE	to rest
	IMPOSE	to place on, as a penalty
	SUPPOSE	to assume to be true
	PROPOSE	to offer, to put forward
	EXPONENT	a person who sets forth or interprets
	POSTPONE	to place later, to delay
	POSIT	to assert, to declare
	POSTURE	(vb) to pose, to assume a fake position (n.) placement of the limbs, carriage

164 | INNOVATOR

NOUN—A person who introduces something new

Google has now become a verb, synonymous with "to search." But Google was not the first to invent the search engine; others preceded Google. However, what made Google **INNOVATIVE** was the PageRank algorithm, which ranks websites on their relevance to a search in order to provide the most useful results. Sergey Brin and Larry Page, the **INNOVATORS** behind Google and PageRank, implemented this algorithm, and the rest is history.

INNOVATE incorporates the Latin root *NOV*, meaning "new." For another use of *NOV*, see Word 51.

165 | STOIC, STOLID

*ADJECTIVE—Seemingly **INDIFFERENT** (Word 113) to or unaffected by joy, grief, pleasure, or pain; impassive and emotionless*

What would you do if you scored the winning goal in a championship soccer game? What would you do if your error caused your team to lose a championship baseball game? Most people would be elated to win and dejected to lose. However, a **STOIC** would remain impassive, showing no emotion in victory or defeat.

Being **STOLID** is not easy. It requires great discipline and self-control. For example, tourists to London are familiar with the distinctive bearskin helmets and scarlet uniforms worn by the guards at Buckingham Palace. The guards are famous for their ability to endure hot summer weather while **STOLIDLY** standing in the same position for hours.

166 | REPROBATE

NOUN—A morally unprincipled person

Who is the most despised **REPROBATE** living in America today? For thousands of betrayed investors there is only one answer—Bernard Madoff. On June 29, 2009, Judge Denny Chin sentenced Madoff to 150 years in prison for running a giant Ponzi scheme that cheated investors out of almost $65 billion. Madoff's victims included pension funds, charitable institutions, and elderly retirees. Although Madoff was a **CHARLATAN** (Word 137), he is best described as a **REPROBATE** because of the enormity of a fraud that Judge Chin called "extraordinarily evil."

CHAPTER 6 REVIEW

Use the word bank below to help complete the sentences. The answer key is on page 143.

Word Bank:

adroit	curtail	dictator	feasible
futile	innovator	obsolete	partisan
placid	squander		

1. Elon Musk is the _____ behind Tesla. Many people consider the Tesla to be the first environmentally friendly sports car.

2. After the joint injury, the baseball player had to _____ his practices and workouts.

3. VHS and cassette tapes are considered _____ technology.

4. The _____ skater landed a quad axel in practice.

5. It is not always _____ to balance work and play.

6. Many citizens believe that _____ politics is the reason our government is so ineffective.

7. The _____ music in the spa room immediately relaxed the client.

8. Lottery winners often hire lawyers and financial advisors before claiming their prize because they want advice on how not to _____ their fortune.

9. During a blizzard, plowing the roads is often _____ because the streets become covered in snow almost as soon as the plow is gone.

10. The evil _____ imprisoned the protesters without a trial.

CHAPTER 7

Pop Words!

Vocabulary in the works of Chaucer and Shakespeare is understandably difficult, but the lyrical stylings of hip hop artists like Aesop Rock often surprise listeners with the amount of unique and obscure script.

See how many of these Pop Words find their way into your next discussion about the latest episode of *Better Call Saul* or into the next singles from Eminem and Kanye.

167 | AMBIVALENT

ADJECTIVE—Having mixed or opposing feelings at the same time

In *The Avengers*, Tony Stark, Steve Rogers, Bruce Banner, and Thor are initially **AMBIVALENT** about joining S.H.I.E.L.D.'s Avenger Initiative. While they know it is necessary to recover the Tesseract from Loki, they fear that their contrasting personalities will be detrimental to the group's success. Thor's **AMBIVALENCE** about working with the Avengers comes from the fact that he is conflicted about fighting his brother Loki.

KNOW YOUR ROOTS		
LATIN PREFIX: ***AMBI*** | both	**AMBIDEXTROUS**	able to use both hands with equal ease, skillful, versatile
	AMBIGUOUS (Word 176)	having two or more possible meanings, doubtful, dubious, **EQUIVOCAL** (Word 26)
	AMBIVALENT	being simultaneously of two minds

168 | ANOMALY

NOUN—Deviation from the norm or what is expected

ANOMALOUS, ATYPICAL

ADJECTIVE—full of ANOMALIES

The Big Bang Theory is a television show that follows the trials and tribulations of an **ATYPICAL** group of friends in Pasadena, California. The group consists of Leonard, an experimental physicist; Sheldon, a theoretical physicist; Howard, an aerospace engineer; Raj, a particle astrophysicist; and Penny, a waitress at The Cheesecake Factory. Can you guess who the **ANOMALY** is? Penny's presence in the group is **ANOMALOUS** for many reasons; besides being a girl, she is trendy and popular and a little **NAÏVE** (Word 184), whereas the men are geeky, **RECLUSIVE** (Word 139), and VERY **ASTUTE** (DH Essential). It's humorous to see these diverse friends spend time together because of their continual disagreements.

169 | PAUCITY

*NOUN—A scarcity or shortage of something; **DEARTH** (DH Essential)*

Critics and moviegoers alike have observed that there is an overall **PAUCITY** of respect for animated features in the Academy Awards. Despite the recent technological and artistic advances in animation, only three animated films have ever been nominated for the **COVETED** (Word 119) Best Picture title: *Beauty and the Beast*, *Up*, and *Toy Story 3*. None of them won the award. Critics were shocked that the phenomenal Pixar film *WALL-E* was not nominated for Best Picture. Though the Academy honors animation through the Best Animated Feature award, industry members speculate that the Best Animated Feature category will perpetuate the **PAUCITY** of animated films nominated for the Best Picture award.

170 | PRATTLE

VERB—To speak in a foolish manner; to babble incessantly

> **PRO TIP**
>
> The word "rattle" is hidden inside of **PRATTLE**. If you remember the baby toy, it can help you to remember how babies **PRATTLE** when they are young: "goo goo, gaa gaa."

Michael Scott of *The Office* served as the regional manager of the Scranton branch of Dunder Mifflin Paper Company. He was most notable, however, for his **INCOHERENT** (Word 66) rambling and often inappropriate remarks. Here is an example of Michael Scott's **PRATTLING** as he discusses his relationship with his employees:

❝*My philosophy is basically this. And this is something that I live by. And I always have. And I always will. Don't ever, for any reason, do anything to anyone, for any reason, ever, no matter what. No matter ... where. Or who, or who you are with, or where you are going, or ... or where you've been ... ever. For any reason, whatsoever.*❞

171 | UNCONVENTIONAL, UNORTHODOX
ADJECTIVE—Not ordinary or typical; characterized by avoiding customary conventions and behaviors

Katy Perry, Lady Gaga, and Nicki Minaj are known for their catchy hits and bold, **UNCONVENTIONAL** wardrobes. The concert film *Katy Perry: Part of Me*, displayed some of Katy's colorful, **UNORTHODOX** costumes, including a dress covered in spinning peppermints, an ice cream cone hat, and a peacock dress.

Lady Gaga is also known for wearing **UNCONVENTIONAL** and even outlandish stage outfits. Some of her most famous **UNORTHODOX** outfits include a coat made of Kermit the Frog dolls and a dress made entirely out of meat.

Some of rapper Nicki Minaj's recent **UNCONVENTIONAL** outfits include a gumball machine-inspired dress and a dress covered in pom-poms. Nicki frequently sports a towering beehive hairstyle, a tribute to Marge Simpson's famous blue beehive.

172 | METICULOUS, PAINSTAKING, FASTIDIOUS
ADJECTIVE—Extremely careful; very exacting

The Wizarding World of Harry Potter at Universal Studios in Florida is a **METICULOUS** re-creation of Hogwarts castle and nearby Hogsmeade village. The park's designers spared no expense to **PAINSTAKINGLY** duplicate such iconic rooms as Dumbledore's office and the Defense Against the Dark Arts classroom. Fascinated visitors can sample butterbeer and even purchase a wand at Ollivander's Wand Shop.

A **FASTIDIOUS** person takes **METICULOUS** to the next level by being overparticular and exacting. Many car owners are **FASTIDIOUS** about keeping their cars spotless.

173 | DIFFIDENT, SELF-EFFACING

ADJECTIVE—Hesitant due to a lack of self-confidence; unassertive; shy; retiring

Many actors and actresses confess to being **DIFFIDENT** in their private lives, despite the fact that they make their livings performing in front of audiences, often in **FLAMBOYANT** (DH Advanced) ways. **SELF-EFFACING** is not what most people think of when they watch Lady Gaga, but apparently even Gaga wakes up feeling insecure and **DIFFIDENT**.

But she then tells herself, "You're Lady Gaga; you get up and walk the walk today."

174 | PRESUMPTUOUS

ADJECTIVE—Taking liberties; brashly overstepping one's place; impertinently bold

One of the most **PRESUMPTUOUS** actions in recent memory occurred during the 2009 *MTV Video Music Awards*. When Taylor Swift came on stage to accept her award for her "You Belong With Me" video, Kanye West appeared and grabbed the microphone out of her hand. He **PRESUMPTUOUSLY** declared, "Taylor, I'm really happy for you. Imma let you finish, but Beyoncé had one of the best videos of all time!" His **AUDACIOUS** (Word 87), arrogant behavior shocked Taylor, Beyoncé, and all who watched the VMAs, and he was widely criticized for it. Eventually, Kanye recognized how **PRESUMPTUOUS** his actions were and made a formal apology.

175 | CLANDESTINE, SURREPTITIOUS

ADJECTIVE—Secret; covert; not open; not aboveboard

Survival during the Zombie Apocalypse on *The Walking Dead* requires a variety of skill sets. Because the walkers are drawn to smell and sound, Rick, Michonne, Darryl, Carol, and the others must traverse the woods in a **CLANDESTINE** manner. **SURREPTITIOUS** movements, such as covering themselves in zombie blood and guts, help shield the survivors against the zombies and other humans.

176 | AMBIGUITY

NOUN—The quality or state of having more than one possible meaning; doubtful; EQUIVOCAL (Word 26)

AMBIGUOUS

ADJECTIVE—Unclear; uncertain; open to more than one interpretation; not definitive; DUBIOUS (DH Essential)

The final scene of the movie *Inception* is full of **AMBIGUITY**. Leo DiCaprio's character, Dom Cobb, is elated because he has found his children and completed the seemingly impossible job he was hired to do. But is all this real or is Dom entrapped in yet another dream? Dom uses a metal top to enable him to determine what is real and what isn't. At the end of the film, Dom spins the top. What will happen next? If the top keeps spinning, Dom is dreaming. If it falls, things are real. We don't know what happens because the ending is deliberately **AMBIGUOUS** (See Know Your Roots, p. 102).

177 | REPROACH, CASTIGATE

NOUN—To express disapproval; to scold; to rebuke

The Tribeca Film Festival, founded by Robert DeNiro, has become one of the preeminent film festivals in the United States. Recently, social media **CASTIGATED** DeNiro and the film festival for a planned screening of the anti-vaccine movie, *Vaxxed*. Even mainstream media outlets and film festival critics **REPROACHED** DeNiro for initially including the documentary in the festival line-up. The main criticism focused on the controversial doctor at the center of the documentary. Utlimately, DeNiro succumbed to disapproval and pulled *Vaxxed* from the festival.

178 | NOSTALGIA

*NOUN—A **WISTFUL** (Word 17) sentimental longing for a place or time in the past*

NOSTALGIC

*ADJECTIVE— Experiencing or exhibiting **NOSTALGIA***

A lifelong fan of The Muppets, Jason Segel was **NOSTALGIC** for his childhood, and he decided to **REJUVENATE** (Word 52) the franchise by writing a new movie for them. Segel said, "We set out to make a Muppet movie that harkened back to the late-'70s, early-'80s Muppets that we grew up with." It's been over a decade since The Muppets starred in a theatrical movie, and, likewise, in *The Muppets*, it's been a while since Kermit and his friends have performed as a group. As the audience revisits their childhood icons during this **NOSTALGIC** film, The Muppets, too, take a **WISTFUL** (Word 17) walk down memory lane. The Muppets decide to get their group together again for one last show, but they discover that they aren't popular anymore. They have become **ANTIQUATED** (Word 144); one character tells them, "You're relics." By incorporating clever humor and **WISTFUL** (Word 17) references to Muppet movies of the past, *The Muppets* introduces a new generation to the **WHIMSICAL** (Word 30) world of Kermit and his friends while also catering to an older **DEMOGRAPHIC's** (DH Advanced) **NOSTALGIA** for their childhood.

179 | GAFFE

NOUN—A blunder; a faux pas; a clumsy social or diplomatic error

The 2012 Olympic Games provided their share of **GAFFES**. Just before the soccer events began, it was learned that the keys to Wembley Stadium had been lost, forcing officials to hastily change all the locks. It appears that the keys had not been stolen, just misplaced.

Then, the North Korean women's soccer team walked off the field at their opening match when organizers mistakenly introduced the players displaying South Korea's flag on the stadium screens. This was a serious *faux pas*: the two countries are still technically at war.

Only after more than an hour's coaxing, humble apologies, and the replacement of South Korea's largely white flag with images of North Korea's red banner did the offended North Korean women agree to take the field.

Another embarrassing blunder occurred when the New Zealand Olympic Committee forgot to register the defending champion, Valerie Adams, for the shot put. The **GAFFE** was spotted before it was too late, and her name was added to the roster.

180 | ANTITHESIS
NOUN—The direct or exact opposite; extreme contrast
ANTITHETICAL
ADJECTIVE—Exactly opposite

Actors often play characters that are the **ANTITHESIS** of who they are in everyday life. Morgan Freeman, a low-key actor who lives in Mississippi rather than Hollywood, has played roles ranging from a chauffeur in *Driving Miss Daisy* to a tech guru in *The Dark Night Trilogy*. Freeman is most known as the voice of God, despite not believing in God. The contrasts between Morgan Freeman's **ANTITHETICAL** characters and who he is as a person underscore his amazing acting ability.

181 | ANTECEDENT, FORERUNNER
NOUN—A preceding event; something that comes before another

Star Wars: The Force Awakens is the highest-grossing film of all time. The film was highly anticipated by avid fans of the **ANTECEDENT**. The original trilogy released in the 1970s and early 1980s developed a cult following and created iconic characters such as Luke Skywalker and Han Solo. Many of the characters that appeared in the 1970s **FORERUNNER** returned in *The Force Awakens*.

KNOW YOUR ROOTS		
GREEK PREFIX:	**ANTEBELLUM**	before the Civil War
ANTE | before	**ANTEDILUVIAN**	before the Biblical flood, a **HYPERBOLIC** (Word 9) word describing something extremely old
	ANTEDATE	to precede in time
	ANTEROOM	a waiting room outside a larger room
	ANTERIOR	before in time and place

182 | IMPLAUSIBLE

*ADJECTIVE–Unbelievable; incredible; not **PLAUSIBLE** (DH Essential)*

PRO TIP

If you add the prefix *im-* to a word, then you negate the meaning of the word because *im-* means NOT. **IMPLAUSIBLE** means NOT **PLAUSIBLE** (DH Essential)!

Let's play **PLAUSIBLE** or **IMPLAUSIBLE**:

In *The Bourne Ultimatum*, Jason Bourne successfully breaks into Noah Vosen's heavily-guarded top-security office and steals an entire set of classified Blackbriar documents. **PLAUSIBLE** or **IMPLAUSIBLE**? **PLAUSIBLE**—because he is Jason Bourne!

In *The Avengers*, Iron Man, Captain America, Thor, The Hulk, Hawkeye, and Black Widow successfully save New York City from an extraterrestrial attack and a nuclear missile. **PLAUSIBLE** or **IMPLAUSIBLE**? **PLAUSIBLE**—because The Avengers all have special skills and powers that allow them to defeat their foes!

183 | ACQUIESCE

VERB–To comply; to agree; to give in

In *Pirates of the Caribbean: The Curse of the Black Pearl*, Elizabeth Swann and Captain Barbossa conduct negotiations that include long words.

Elizabeth Swann:	Captain Barbossa, I am here to negotiate the cessation of hostilities against Port Royal.
Captain Barbossa:	There be a lot of long words in there, Miss. We're naught but humble pirates. What is it that you want?
Elizabeth Swann:	I want you to leave and never come back.
Captain Barbossa:	I'm disinclined to **ACQUIESCE** to your request. Means no!

Although he is a "humble pirate," Captain Barbossa can use long words as well as she can.

184 | NAÏVE, GULLIBLE

ADJECTIVE–Unaffectedly simple; lacking worldly expertise; unsophisticated; immature; inexperienced; INGENUOUS (DH Advanced)

Nemo, of *Finding Nemo*, is a young clownfish who thinks he is old enough to swim out in the open waters. Young, **NAÏVE**, and wanting to defy his overprotective father, he wanders too near a boat. Suddenly, a net surrounds him. He is taken aboard the boat and from there to Sydney, Australia, to live in a fish tank. His father, Marlin, **DESPONDENT** (Word 57) at his loss, vows to find his son. Marlin succeeds and ultimately brings Nemo back home. By the end of the film, Nemo has learned the importance of obeying his father and of not being so **GULLIBLE**.

185 | UBIQUITOUS, PREVALENT, PERVASIVE

ADJECTIVE–Characterized by being everywhere; omnipresent; widespread

What do smart phones, tablets, Starbucks coffee shops, and McDonald's fast-food restaurants have in common? They are all **UBIQUITOUS**— we see them everywhere. Popular fashions are also **PERVASIVE**. For example, baggy knee-length shorts have completely replaced the once-**PREVALENT** short shorts of the 1970s. From high school b-ballers to WNBA and NBA superstars, long shorts are now **UBIQUITOUS**.

186 | DIMINUTIVE
ADJECTIVE—Very small

Certain sports, like basketball and football, rely on the size and strength of players in order to win. However, gymnastics and horse racing feature **DIMINUTIVE** athletes. The average height of a female Olympic gymnastic medalist is 5 feet 1 inch. Additionally, champion gymnasts weigh around 100 pounds. The **DIMINUTIVE** frame of female gymnasts allows them to maintain a high strength-to-weight ratio. This ratio enables the gymnasts to perform astounding feats of strength, agility, and precision. Correspondingly, the most successful jockeys in horse racing and steeplechase are **DIMINUTIVE**. For each race, the racing authorities set limits for the amount of weight each horse can carry, which includes the equipment. Therefore, jockeys must be **DIMINUTIVE** in order for the horse to meet the weight requirements. Jockeys typically weigh between 108 and 118 pounds and stand between 4 feet 10 inches and 5 feet 6 inches tall.

187 | TRIVIAL
ADJECTIVE—Trifling; unimportant; insignificant

MINUTIAE
NOUN—Minor everyday details

Drake is one of the world's most popular hip hop artists. While Drake would prefer to concentrate on creating music, his **ZEALOUS** (DH Essential) fans often focus on interesting but **TRIVIAL MINUTIAE** about his personal life. For example, Drake was raised by a Jewish mother and had a Bar Mitzvah. And online rumors continue to link him with Rihanna!

188 | EXHORT

VERB—To encourage; to urge; to give a pep talk; to IMPLORE (DH Essential)

American League baseball player Derek Jeter spent his entire career with the New York Yankees. Naturally, New York fans love him. When Jeter began to approach the **COVETED** (Word 119) 3,000 hit milestone, his teammates and fans **EXHORTED** him to continue to play well so he could reach the **ELUSIVE** (Word 42) milestone. The **EXHORTATIONS** worked. On July 9, 2011, he became the first New York Yankee to reach the 3,000 hit mark. Even sweeter, his 3,000th hit was a home run!

189 | ANTIPATHY, ENMITY, RANCOR

NOUN—Strong dislike; ill will; the state of detesting someone

Many reality television shows' plot lines are driven by the **ANTIPATHY** between cast members. The *Real Housewives* franchise showcases the disagreements and **ENMITY** the cast have for each other. Whether New York City, Beverly Hills, or Atlanta, it is clear that the producers encourage the **RANCOR** between the women because their bitter feuds bring higher ratings and make headlines.

190 | DIGRESS

VERB—To depart from a subject; to wander; to ramble

Have you ever listened to someone who repeatedly wanders off a topic? If so, then you know how confusing and annoying it is when a speaker **DIGRESSES** from a subject. In the movie *Office Space*, Milton is **NOTORIOUS** (DH Essential) for his long-winded **DIGRESSIONS**. **DIGRESSING** is not limited to speaking. Writers sometimes **DIGRESS** or wander off a topic. Some standardized tests require essays. Readers reward essays that are well-organized and deduct points from essays that **DIGRESS** from the topic.

KNOW YOUR ROOTS

LATIN ROOT:	PROGRESS	to step forward
GRESS | to step	REGRESS	to step back
	TRANSGRESS	to step across the line that divides right from wrong
	EGRESS	to step out, to exit (or as a noun, an exit)
	AGGRESSIVE	tending to attack, encroach, or step on others

191 | TENACIOUS

ADJECTIVE—Characterized by holding fast to something valued; showing great determination

PRO TIP

The root of **TENACIOUS** is the Latin root *TEN*, "to hold." You can find it in **TENET**, an opinion, idea, or principle HELD true by a person or organization. It's also in **TENABLE**, which means capable of being HELD, defended, and logically supported, as in a **TENABLE** argument or thesis.

JJ Watt is one of the most **TENACIOUS** professional football players on the field today. His exercise regimen and work ethic are well-known among his teammates and his fans. The Houston Texans defensive end wakes up at 3:45 in the morning to begin his day. He completely dedicates himself to his fitness and football training. After a long day of workouts and practice, Watt tries to be in bed no later than 7:30 pm. Sometimes teased for his strict schedule, Watt explained his logic:

"The way I look at it is that somebody in the world, no matter what your field is—teacher, violinist, football player—has to be the best. Why not me? If I dedicate all my time, if I cut out all the other crap from my life, if I give everything I have to this game for 10 or 12 years, maybe it is. And when I'm done, I'll go sit on my front porch with my buddies, have a beer, and say, `That was pretty cool, wasn't it?"

192 | INDULGENT
ADJECTIVE—Characterized by excessive generosity; overly tolerant

The Kardashian and Jenner families are **INFAMOUS** (DH Essential) for their **LAVISH** (DH Essential) lifestyle. Kris Jenner is often **CASTIGATED** (Word 177) for her **INDULGENT** parenting style. She has allowed all of her daughters to live a life of excess and market it on social media. Whether it is new cars, new clothes, or new boyfriends, Kim, Khloe, Kourtney, Kendall, and Kylie are permitted to spend what they want and do what they want with virtually no limits.

193 | EPHEMERAL, FLEETING, EVANESCENT
ADJECTIVE—Very brief; lasting for a short time; transient

PERENNIAL
ADJECTIVE—Returning year after year; enduring

What do the following groups and their hit songs have in common: "Who Let the Dogs Out?" by Baha Men, "Stuck In The Middle With You" by Stealers Wheel, and "It's Raining Men" by the Weather Girls? All three groups were "one-hit wonders" who had a single hit song and then disappeared. Their popularity was **EVANESCENT**. They were **EPHEMERAL**—here today and gone tomorrow.

On the contrary, bands like The Beatles, The Beach Boys, and Simon & Garfunkel have remained **PERENNIAL** favorites. The Beatles' albums continue to be bestsellers on iTunes. The Beach Boys still maintain a busy tour schedule, and the songs of Simon & Garfunkel remain staples of popular culture. Paul Simon was even asked to perform their hit song "The Sound of Silence" at the 9/11 tenth anniversary memorial service. All three of these bands have maintained immense popularity throughout the decades.

194 | PENCHANT, PREDILECTION, PROPENSITY

*NOUN—A liking or preference for something; a **BENT** (DH Advanced); an inclination*

Gossip magazines and blogs are **CAPRICIOUS** in nature toward the celebrities they cover. One minute they **LAMBASTED** (DH Advanced) Blake Shelton for partying too much and leaving Miranda Lambert alone. Only weeks later, the **FICKLE** (Word 195) press attacked Miranda Lambert for **ALLEGEDLY** (DH Essential) cheating on Shelton. Finally, the **MERCURIAL** (Word 195) gossip pages published sympathetic articles about Lambert leaving the Oklahoma farm she shared with Shelton after the divorce papers were filed.

195 | CAPRICIOUS, MERCURIAL, FICKLE

ADJECTIVE—Very changeable; characterized by constantly shifting moods

When the gossip magazine *Us Weekly* published a story and photos of *Twilight*'s Kristen Stewart cheating on her boyfriend Robert Pattinson, passionate *Twilight* fans responded in disbelief on their Twitter accounts. The outraged fans **LAMBASTED** (DH Advanced) the magazine and insisted that the photos of Stewart were fake. However, Stewart released a statement apologizing for her "momentary indiscretion" and declaring her love for Pattinson. The **FICKLE** fans turned **CAPRICIOUSLY** from supporting Stewart to **CASTIGATING** (Word 177) her and mourning the end of their favorite celebrity couple. Fans added **MAUDLIN** (DH Advanced) videos and social media posts online, expressing shock over the breakup of "Robsten."

MEDIEVAL HUMOURS

In medieval times, it was believed that people's personalities or moods were determined by the relative amounts of the four bodily fluids (or HUMOURS) in their bodies. Though we no longer believe in the physiological basis, we still use the words to describe people.

Predominant Fluid	Temperament	Aspects
Blood	**SANGUINE** (DH Advanced)	cheerful, hopeful, optimistic
Black bile	**MELANCHOLY** (DH Essential)	gloomy, depressed, **DESPONDENT** (Word 57), **PENSIVE** (Word 25)
Yellow bile	**CHOLERIC**	angry, irritable, **IRASCIBLE**
Phlegm	**PHLEGMATIC**	self-possessed, imperturbable, calm, **APATHETIC** (DH Essential), sluggish
Fluctuating among all four fluids	**MERCURIAL** (Word 195)	volatile, changeable, **FICKLE** (Word 195)

196 | BOORISH, UNCOUTH, CRASS

ADJECTIVE—Vulgar; characterized by crude behavior and deplorable manners; unrefined

Games of Thrones originated from a very popular series of fantasy novels written by George R.R. Martin. In 2011, HBO developed the books into a serial drama. Before the show aired, rumors of the **BOORISH** nature of the storylines were discussed in the press. The violent and sexually explicit content was thought to be too **CRASS** for viewers. On the contrary, *Game of Thrones* has received critical and fan praise despite the **UNCOUTH** actions of its characters.

197 | INNUENDO

NOUN—A veiled reference; an insinuation

At the beginning of *The Godfather,* Kay does not understand the workings of the Corleone family business, and she asks Michael how his father managed a business deal. Michael responds with an **INNUENDO**: "My father made him an offer he couldn't refuse." His response insinuates that Don Vito uses **COERCION** (DH Advanced) and threats in his business dealings. Michael's **INNUENDO** suggests that his father is a powerful mob boss.

198 | VORACIOUS, RAVENOUS, INSATIABLE

ADJECTIVE—Having a huge appetite that cannot be satisfied

What do Homer (*The Simpsons*), Bluto (*Animal House*), and Scooby-Doo (*Scooby Do! Mystery Incorporated*) have in common? All three have **VORACIOUS** appetites. Homer has an **INSATIABLE** appetite for frosted doughnuts. Bluto regularly and **BOORISHLY** (Word 196) piles great quantities of food on his plate. Scooby has a **RAVENOUS** appetite for Scooby Snacks, and he habitually sneaks food from the plates of his friends.

199 | POIGNANT

ADJECTIVE—Moving; touching; heartrending

In the movie *Remember the Titans,* Gerry Bertier and Julius Campbell are forced to become teammates on the racially-divided T.C. Williams High School football team. Although originally bitter rivals, they overcome their prejudices and become close friends. When Julius visits the paralyzed Gerry in the hospital, the nurse bars Julius, who is black, from the room, saying, "Only kin's allowed in here." But Gerry corrects her: "Alice, are you blind? Don't you see the family resemblance? That's my brother." This **POIGNANT** scene brought tears to the eyes of many viewers.

200 | DISPEL

*VERB—To drive away; scatter, as to **DISPEL** a misconception*

Hollywood actors and actresses have to deal with stories about their private lives, both true and false, in the press. Because image is vital to success in Hollywood, celebrities employ public relations firms to handle their press. **DISPELLING** rumors is one of the jobs of a public relations agent. Whether it is an unnamed resource suggesting that an actress is cheating on her husband or a photograph of an actor gambling to excess in Las Vegas, the public relations agent will arrange for the accused celebrity to visit sick children at a hospital or set up a photo opportunity making it look as though the actress is happily married. Depending on the person, it can be a full-time job for someone to **DISPEL** all the rumors.

201 | INTEMPERATE

ADJECTIVE—Lacking restraint; excessive

TEMPERATE

ADJECTIVE—Exercising moderation and restraint

INTEMPERATE habits such as smoking, drinking, and overeating are harmful to good health. In contrast, a **TEMPERATE** person leads a lifestyle characterized by moderation and self-restraint. Bluto (*Animal House*), Frank "The Tank" (*Old School*), and Ben Stone (*Knocked Up*) were all fun-loving, **INTEMPERATE** party animals. Compare their lifestyles to Andy Stitzer's (*The 40-Year-Old Virgin*) far more **TEMPERATE** approach to life.

The 18th century British author Samuel Johnson is famed for saying, "Abstinence is as easy to me as **TEMPERANCE** would be difficult."

202 | LAUD, EXTOL, TOUT, ACCLAIM

VERB—To praise; to applaud

PRO TIP

LAUDS is the morning church service in which psalms of praise to God are sung. Note that the word appLAUD contains the root word **LAUD. LAUD** and its synonyms **EXTOL**, **TOUT**, and **ACCLAIM** all mean to praise.

What do The Beach Boys' classic song "California Girls" and Katy Perry's hit "California Gurls" have in common? Both songs **EXTOL** the beauty of California girls. The Beach Boys acknowledge that they are captivated by the way southern girls talk. They **LAUD** east coast girls for being hip. However, this doesn't shake their belief that California girls are "the cutest girls in the world."

Needless to say, Katy Perry agrees with The Beach Boys. She proudly **TOUTS** the beauty of California's **ACCLAIMED** golden coast. But that is not all. The California boys "break their necks" trying to sneak a peek at the "California gurls." According to Katy, "California gurls" wear "unforgettable Daisy Dukes, bikinis on top."

203 | DISPARAGE

VERB—To speak of in a slighting or disrespectful way; to belittle

Carolina Panthers' quarterback Cam Newton was given the nickname Superman during the 2015 football season. He was outspoken about his team's dominance and rarely shied away from cameras, so his post-game Super Bowl press conference generated criticism. Contrary to his **BRASH** (DH Essential) persona before the loss, Newton was slumped in a chair with a hoodie pulled over his face. After a few minutes, he said he was done and walked away. Newton was **DISPARAGED** across social media platforms for his "cry baby" attitude. Even actor Rob Lowe **SARDONICALLY** (Word 85) tweeted:

"*Wow. What a press conference from Cam Newton. So gracious! So classy! What an example to kids! Just like Peyton.***"**

204 | MENTOR

NOUN—An advisor; a teacher; a guide

ACOLYTE

NOUN—A devoted follower

In the *Star Wars* **SAGA** (Word 11), Obi-Wan Kenobi is a Jedi Knight who serves as Luke Skywalker's **MENTOR**. As an eager young **ACOLYTE** of the **SAGE** (Word 122) Kenobi, Skywalker learns the ways of the Force, a natural power harnessed by the Jedi in their struggle against the **NEFARIOUS** (DH Advanced) Darth Vader and the evil Galactic Empire.

205 | BUNGLER

NOUN—Someone who is clumsy or INEPT; a person who makes mistakes because of incompetence

INEPT

ADJECTIVE—Incompetent, clumsy, or careless; having or showing no skill

BUNGLERS have been featured in a number of movies. For example, in the movie *21 Jump Street*, officers Morton Schmidt and Greg Jenko are **BUNGLERS** who botch their investigations and police work. They forget to read the Miranda rights to a criminal during an arrest, confuse their undercover identities, and even get fired from the Jump Street division for their **INEPT** work.

In the movie *The Princess Diaries*, Mia Thermopolis is a **BUNGLER** who is **INEPT** in social situations, awkward and clumsy. However, she discovers that she's the princess of Genovia, a small European country. After taking many "Princess Lessons," she emerges as a confident princess, fit to rule her country.

206 | PUNDIT

*NOUN—An expert commentator; an **AUTHORITY** (DH Essential) who expresses his or her opinion, usually on political issues*

From CNN's News Center to ESPN's Sports Center, television programs are filled with **PUNDITS** who offer their "expert" commentary on issues ranging from political campaigns to March Madness brackets. The **PUNDITS** almost always sound authoritative and convincing, but it is wise to maintain a healthy **SKEPTICISM** (DH Essential). Here are expert opinions from famous pundits who turned out to be wrong:

"Louis Pasteur's theory of germs is ridiculous fiction."
Pierre Packet, Professor of Physiology at Toulouse, 1872

"Heavier-than-air flying machines are impossible."
Lord Kelvin, President of the Royal Society, 1895

"Stocks have reached what looks like a permanently high plateau."
Irving Fisher, Professor of Economics, Yale University, 1929

"There is no reason anyone would want a computer in their home."
Ken Olson, President, Chairman, and Founder of Digital Equipment Corp., 1977

207 | NEOPHYTE, GREENHORN

*NOUN—A beginner; someone new to a field or activity; **NOVICE** (DH Essential)*

In October 2008, Justin Bieber was an unknown **NEOPHYTE** who had never professionally recorded a song. However, Usher recognized that although Bieber was a **NOVICE**, he was a musical **PRODIGY** (Word 141) with the potential to become a superstar. With Usher as his **MENTOR** (Word 204), Bieber quickly transformed from a **GREENHORN** into a global sensation. No longer a **NOVICE**, Bieber has begun **MENTORING** and promoting other musical **GREENHORNS**. After hearing Carly Rae Jepsen's song "Call Me Maybe," he tweeted about the song and convinced his manager to sign the Canadian singer. "Call Me Maybe" became the source of numerous **PARODIES** (Word 8) that were very popular and became a major hit.

CHAPTER 7 REVIEW

Complete each word box. The answer key is on page 143.

Extremely careful:

Word 1: _____

Word 2: _____

Word 3: _____

Characterized by crude behavior:

Word 1: _____

Word 2: _____

Word 3: _____

Ambivalent:
Definition in your own words: _____

_____

_____

Nostalgia:
Definition in your own words: _____

_____

_____

Gullible:
List 3 synonyms: _____

Trivial:
List 3 synonyms: _____

Tenacious:
List 3 synonyms: _____

Fickle:
List 3 synonyms: _____

Poignant:
Use the word in a sentence that helps explain what it means.

_____

_____

Mentor:
Use the word in a sentence that helps explain what it means.

_____

_____

Fast Review

CHAPTER 1: RHETORICAL/LITERARY TERMS

1. **FIGURATIVE/METAPHORICAL LANGUAGE** *(n.)*—A general term referring to language that describes a thing in terms of something else. The resemblance is **FIGURATIVE** (DH Essential), not **LITERAL** (DH Essential), as the reader is carried beyond the **LITERAL** meaning to consider the **NUANCES** (DH Advanced) and connotations of the words used in the comparison.

2. **SIMILE** *(n.)*—A clearly stated figure of speech that is a comparison between two essentially unlike things, usually using the words "like" or "as," which points out a **FIGURATIVE** (DH Essential) way that the two things ARE alike.

3. **METAPHOR** *(n.)*—In its more narrow sense, a figure of speech in which one thing is described in terms of another using an implied comparison, without the use of "like" or "as."

4. **PERSONIFICATION** *(n.)*—A figure of speech in which an inanimate object is given human qualities or abilities

5. **PARALLELISM/PARALLEL STRUCTURE** *(n.)*—A rhetorical device or sentence construction which involves using matching grammatical patterns to establish the equivalent relationship or importance of two or more items. **PARALLELISM** provides balance and **AUTHORITY** (DH Essential) to sentences.

6. **IRONIC** *(adj.)*—Using words to convey a meaning that is the opposite of its literal meaning
   IRONICALLY *(adv.)*—Pertaining to, exhibiting, or characterized by mockery

7. **SYNOPSIS** *(n.)*—A brief summary of the major points of a thesis, theory, story, or literary work; an abstract

8. **SATIRE, LAMPOON, PARODY** *(n.)*—A work that ridicules human vices, follies, and foibles; comic criticism.
   SATIRIZE, LAMPOON, PARODY *(v.)*—To ridicule or mock, often **SARCASTICALLY** (DH Essential)

9. **HYPERBOLE** *(n.)*—A figure of speech in which exaggeration is used for emphasis or effect; extreme exaggeration

10. **CARICATURE** *(n.)*—Visual art or descriptive writing that deliberately exaggerates distinctive features or peculiarities of a subject for comic or absurd effect

11. **EPIC** *(n.)*—A long narrative poem written in a grand style to celebrate the feats of a legendary hero
EPIC *(adj.)*—Grand, sweeping, or of historical or legendary importance
SAGA *(n.)*—A long narrative story; a heroic tale

12. **FORESHADOWING** *(v.)*—A suggestion or indication that something will happen in a story; a hint that **PRESAGES** (DH Advanced)

13. **ANECDOTE** *(n.)*—A short account of an interesting or humorous incident

14. **EULOGY** *(n.)*—A **LAUDATORY** (Word 202) speech or written tribute, especially one praising someone who has died

15. **ALLUSION** *(n.)*—An indirect or brief reference to a person, event, place, phrase, piece of art, or literary work that assumes a common knowledge with the reader or listener

16. **ANALOGY** *(n.)*—A similarity or likeness between things—events, ideas, actions, trends—that are otherwise unrelated
ANALOGOUS *(adj.)*—Comparable or similar in certain respects

CHAPTER 2: NAME THAT TONE/WATCH THAT ATTITUDE

17. **WISTFUL** *(adj.)*—Longing and yearning, tinged with **MELANCHOLY** (DH Essential) and **PENSIVENESS** (Word 25)

18. **EARNEST, SINCERE** *(adj.)*—Serious in intention or purpose; showing depth and genuine feelings

19. **DISGRUNTLED, DISCONTENTED** *(adj.)*—Angry; dissatisfied; annoyed; impatient; irritated

20. **AUTHORITATIVE** *(adj.)*—Commanding and self-confident; likely to be respected and obeyed, based on competent **AUTHORITY** (DH Essential)

21. **FRIVOLITY** *(n.)*—The trait of being **FRIVOLOUS**; not serious or sensible
FRIVOLOUS *(adj.)*—Lacking any serious purpose or value; given to trifling or levity

22. **ACERBIC, ACRID** *(adj.)*—Harsh, bitter, sharp, **CAUSTIC** (DH Advanced)

23. **SOLEMN, SOMBER** *(adj.)*—Not cheerful or smiling; serious; gloomy; **GRAVE** (DH Essential)

24. **INQUISITIVE** *(adj.)*—Curious; inquiring

25. **REFLECTIVE, PENSIVE** *(adj.)*—Engaged in, involving, or reflecting deep or serious thought, usually marked by sadness or **MELANCHOLY** (DH Essential)

26. **EQUIVOCAL** *(adj.)*—**AMBIGUOUS** (Word 176), open to interpretation, having several equally possible meanings
    EQUIVOCATE *(v.)*—To avoid making an explicit statement; to hedge; to use vague or AMBIGUOUS (see KNOW YOUR ROOTS, p. 102) language

27. **DEFERENTIAL** *(adj.)*—Respectful; dutiful

28. **EBULLIENT, EUPHORIC** *(adj.)*—Feeling or expressing great happiness or triumph; elated

29. **MALEVOLENT** *(adj.)*—Wishing evil to others, showing ill will
    BENEVOLENT (DH Essential) *(adj.)*—Well-meaning; kindly

30. **WHIMSICAL** *(adj.)*—Playful; fanciful; **CAPRICIOUS** (Word 195); given to whimsies or odd notions

31. **PROSAIC, MUNDANE** *(adj.)*—Dull; uninteresting; ordinary; commonplace; tedious; **PEDESTRIAN** (DH Advanced); **VAPID** (DH Advanced); **BANAL** (Word 121); **HACKNEYED** (DH Advanced); unexceptional

32. **VITRIOLIC** *(adj.)*—Bitter; **CAUSTIC** (DH Advanced); **ACERBIC** (Word 22); filled with malice

33. **CONCILIATORY** *(adj.)*—Appeasing; intending to **PLACATE** (DH Advanced)

34. **DESPAIRING** *(adj.)*—Showing the loss of all hope

35. **INFLAMMATORY** *(adj.)*—Arousing; intended to inflame a situation or ignite angry or violent feelings

36. **NONCHALANT** *(adj.)*—Having an air of casual indifference; coolly unconcerned; **UNFLAPPABLE**

CHAPTER 3: LET'S BREAK IT DOWN!

37. **EXPUNGE, EXCISE, EXPURGATE** *(v.)*—To take OUT; to delete; to remove

38. **ECCENTRIC** *(adj.)*—Literally OUT of the center; departing from a recognized, conventional, or established norm; an odd, **UNCONVENTIONAL** (Word 171) person

39. **EXTRICATE** *(v.)*—To get OUT of a difficult situation or entanglement

40. **EXEMPLARY** *(adj.)*—Standing OUT from the norm; outstanding; worthy of imitation

41. **ENUMERATE** *(v.)*—To count OUT; to list; to tick off the reasons for

42. **ELUSIVE** *(adj.)*—OUT of reach and therefore difficult to catch, define, or describe

43. **EXORBITANT** *(adj.)*—Literally OUT of orbit and therefore unreasonably expensive

44. **REDUNDANT** *(adj.)*—Needlessly repetitive; saying things AGAIN and AGAIN

45. **REPUDIATE, RECANT, RENOUNCE** *(v.)*—To take BACK; to reject; to disavow

46. **RELINQUISH** *(v.)*—To surrender or give back (or return) a possession, right, or privilege

47. **RESILIENT** *(adj.)*—Bouncing BACK from adversity or misfortune; recovering quickly
    RESILIENCE *(n.)*—The ability to recover from adversity

48. **REAFFIRM** *(v.)*—To assert AGAIN; to confirm; to state positively

49. **RETICENT** *(adj.)*—Holding BACK one's thoughts, feelings and personal affairs; restrained or reserved

50. **REBUFF** *(v.)*—To repel or drive BACK; to bluntly reject

51. **RENOVATE** *(v.)*—To make new AGAIN; to restore by repairing and remodeling

52. **REJUVENATE** *(v.)*—To make young AGAIN; to restore youthful vigor and appearance

53. **RESURGENT** *(adj.)*—Rising AGAIN; sweeping or surging BACK

54. **REPUGNANT** *(adj.)*—Offensive to the mind or senses; causing distaste or aversion; abhorrent

55. **DELETERIOUS** *(adj.)*—Going DOWN in the sense of having a harmful effect; injurious

56. **DECRY** *(v.)*—To put DOWN in the sense of openly condemning; to express strong disapproval

57. **DESPONDENT, MOROSE** *(adj.)*—**DOWNCAST** (DH Essential); very dejected; **FORLORN** (DH Essential)

58. **DENOUNCE** *(v.)*—To put DOWN in the sense of a making a formal accusation; to speak against

59. **DEMISE** *(n.)*—Sent DOWN in the sense of ending in death; the cessation of existence or activity

60. **DEBUNK** *(v.)*—To put DOWN by exposing false and exaggerated claims

61. **DERIDE, DERISION** *(v.)*—To put DOWN with contemptuous jeering; to ridicule or laugh at
    DERISIVE *(adj.)*—Characterized by or expressing contempt; mocking
    DERISION *(n.)*—The act of mockery; ridicule

62. **DEVOID, BEREFT** *(adj.)*—DOWN in the sense of being empty; completely lacking in substance or quality; vacant

63. **IMPECCABLE** *(adj.)*—Having NO flaws; perfect

64. **IMPLACABLE** *(adj.)*—NOT capable of being **PLACATED** (DH Advanced) or appeased

65. **INEXORABLE** *(adj.)*—NOT capable of being stopped; relentless; inevitable

66. **INCOHERENT** *(adj.)*—NOT coherent and therefore lacking organization; lacking logical or meaningful connections

67. **INSURMOUNTABLE** *(adj.)*—NOT capable of being surmounted or overcome

68. **IRREVERENT** *(adj.)*—Lacking proper respect or seriousness; disrespectful

69. **IRRESOLUTE** *(adj.)*—NOT **RESOLUTE** (DH Advanced); uncertain how to act or proceed; indecisive; **VACILLATING** (DH Advanced)

70. **CIRCUMSPECT** *(adj.)*—Looking carefully around—thus cautious and careful; **PRUDENT** (DH Advanced); discreet

71. **CIRCUITOUS** *(adj.)*—CIRCULAR and therefore indirect in language, behavior, or action, roundabout

72. **CIRCUMVENT** *(v.)*—To circle AROUND and therefore bypass; to avoid by artful maneuvering

73. **CIRCUMSCRIBE** *(v.)*—To draw a line AROUND and therefore to narrowly limit or restrict actions

74. **MAGNANIMOUS** *(adj.)*—FILLED WITH generosity and forgiveness; forgoing resentment and revenge

75. **ERRONEOUS** *(adj.)*—FILLED WITH errors; wrong

76. **MOMENTOUS** *(adj.)*—FILLED WITH importance; very significant

77. **MELLIFLUOUS** *(adj.)*—Smooth and sweet; flowing like honey

78. **ACRIMONIOUS, RANCOROUS** *(adj.)*—Filled with bitterness; sharpness in words

79. **COPIOUS** *(adj.)*—FILLED WITH abundance; plentiful

80. **ABSTEMIOUS** *(adj.)*—FILLED WITH moderation; **TEMPERATE** (Word 201) in eating and drinking

81. **MALODOROUS** *(adj.)*—FILLED WITH an unpleasant odor; foul-smelling

82. **HEINOUS, EGREGIOUS** *(adj.)*—Flagrantly, conspicuously bad; abominable; shockingly evil; monstrous; outrageous

83. **GRATUITOUS** *(adj.)*—Unwarranted; not called for by the circumstances; unnecessary

84. **PRECARIOUS, PERILOUS** *(adj.)*—Uncertain; characterized by a lack of security or stability

CHAPTER 4: SOMETIMES HISTORY REPEATS ITSELF

85. **SARDONIC, SNIDE** *(adj.)*—Mocking; derisive; taunting; stinging; **SARCASTIC** (DH Essential)

86. **WRY, DROLL** *(adj.)*—Dry; humorous with a clever twist and a touch of irony

87. **AUDACIOUS** *(adj.)*—Fearlessly, often recklessly daring; very bold

88. **PRAGMATIC** *(adj.)*—Practical; sensible; NOT idealistic or romantic

89. **EVOCATION** *(n.)*—An imaginative re-creation of something; a calling forth
    EVOKE *(v.)*—To call or to summon something, especially from the past

90. **AFFABLE, GENIAL, GREGARIOUS** *(adj.)*—Agreeable; marked by a pleasing personality; warm and friendly; **AMIABLE** (DH Essential)

91. **AUSTERE** *(adj.)*—Having no adornment or ornamentation; bare; not **ORNATE** (DH Advanced)
    AUSTERITY *(n.)*—Great self-denial, economy, discipline; lack of adornment

92. **ALTRUISM** *(n.)*—Unselfish concern for the welfare of others

93. **AUSPICIOUS, PROPITIOUS** *(adj.)*—Very favorable

94. **MITIGATE, MOLLIFY, ALLEVIATE** *(v.)*—To relieve; to lessen; to ease

95. **FORTITUDE** *(n.)*—Strength of mind that allows one to endure pain or adversity with courage

96. **POLARIZE** *(v.)*—To create disunity or dissension; to break up into opposing factions or groups; to be divisive

97. **THWART, STYMIE** *(v.)*—To stop; to frustrate; to prevent

98. **INTREPID, UNDAUNTED** *(adj.)*—Courageous; **RESOLUTE** (DH Advanced); fearless

99. **ITINERANT** *(adj.)*—Migrating from place to place; NOT **SEDENTARY** (DH Advanced)

100. **IMPETUS** *(n.)*—A stimulus or encouragement that results in increased activity

101. **EQUANIMITY** *(n.)*—Calmness; composure; even-temperedness; poise

102. **PROVOCATIVE** *(adj.)*—Provoking discussion; stimulating controversy; arousing a reaction

103. **FORTUITOUS** *(adj.)*—Of accidental but fortunate occurrence; having unexpected good fortune

104. **RHETORICIAN** *(n.)*—An eloquent writer or speaker
    RHETORIC *(n.)*—The art of speaking and writing

105. **HEDONIST** *(n.)*—A person who believes that pleasure is the chief goal of life

106. **ASCETIC** *(n.)*—A person who gives up material comforts and leads a life of self-denial, especially as an act of religious devotion

107. **RACONTEUR** *(n.)*—A person who excels in telling **ANECDOTES** (DH Advanced)

108. **ICONOCLAST** *(n.)*—A person who attacks and ridicules cherished figures, ideas, and institutions

109. **DEMAGOGUE** *(n.)*—A leader who appeals to the fears, emotions, and prejudices of the populace

110. **ORACLE** *(n.)*—A person considered to be a source of wise counsel or prophetic opinions

111. **SYCOPHANT** *(n.)*—A person who seeks favor by flattering people of influence; someone who behaves in an **OBSEQUIOUS** (DH Advanced) or **SERVILE** (DH Advanced) manner

112. **RENEGADE** *(n.)*—A disloyal person who betrays his or her cause; a traitor; a deserter

CHAPTER 5: ART AND LITERATURE IN CONTEXT

113. **INDIFFERENT** *(adj.)*—Marked by a lack of interest or concern; **NONCHALANT** (Word 36); **APATHETIC** (DH Essential)

114. **RECALCITRANT, OBSTINATE, OBDURATE** *(adj.)*—Stubbornly resistant and defiant; **REFRACTORY** (DH Advanced); disobedient

115. **BOON** *(n.)*—A timely benefit; blessing
     BANE *(n.)*—A source of harm and ruin

116. **IMPASSE** *(n.)*—A deadlock; stalemate; failure to reach an agreement

117. **ANACHRONISM** *(n.)*—The false assignment of an event, person, scene, or language to a time when the event, person, scene, or word did not exist

118. **BELIE** *(v.)*—To contradict; to prove false, appearances that are mis-representative

119. **COVET** *(v.)*—To strongly desire; to crave
     COVETOUS *(adj.)*—Grasping, greedy, eager to obtain something; **AVARICIOUS** (DH Advanced)

120. **ALOOF** *(adj.)*—Reserved or quiet; disinterested
     ALOOF *(adv.)*—Detached; distant physically or emotionally; standing near but apart

121. **TRITE, BANAL, INSIPID** *(adj.)*—Unoriginal; commonplace; overused; **CLICHÉD** (DH Essential)

122. **SAGE** *(adj.)*—Profoundly wise or prudent

123. **AESTHETIC** *(adj.)*—Relating to the nature of beauty, art, and taste; having a sense of what is beautiful, attractive, or pleasing
     AESTHETICALLY *(adv.)*—According to **AESTHETICS** or its principles and manner

124. **PARADOX** *(n.)*—A seemingly contradictory statement that, nonetheless, expresses a truth

125. **ENIGMATIC, INSCRUTABLE** *(adj.)*—Mysterious; puzzling; unfathomable; baffling

126. **AUTONOMY** *(n.)*—Independence; self-governance
     AUTONOMOUS *(adj.)*—Acting independently, or having the freedom to do so; not controlled by others

127. **NEBULOUS** *(adj.)*—Vague; cloudy; misty; lacking a fully-developed form

128. **BEREFT** *(adj.)*—Deprived of or lacking something

129. **CALLOUS** *(adj.)*—Emotionally hardened; insensitive; unfeeling

130. **BUCOLIC, RUSTIC, PASTORAL** *(adj.)*—Characteristic of charming, un-spoiled countryside and the simple, rural life

131. **ANGUISH** *(n.)*—Agonizing physical or mental pain; torment

132. **SUPERFICIAL** *(adj.)*—Shallow; lacking in depth; concerned with surface appearances

133. **DISMISSIVE** *(adj.)*—Showing overt intentional **INDIFFERENCE** (Word 113) or disregard; rejecting

134. **POMPOUS, PRETENTIOUS** *(adj.)*—Filled with excessive self-importance; **OSTENTATIOUS** (DH Essential); boastful

135. **CRYPTIC** *(adj.)*—Having a hidden or **AMBIGUOUS** (Word 176) meaning; mysterious

136. **SUBTLE** *(adj.)*—Difficult to detect; faint; mysterious; likely to elude perception

137. **CHARLATAN** *(n.)*—A fake; fraud; imposter; cheat

138. **BUFFOON** *(n.)*—A person who amuses others with odd behavior and jokes; clown; jester; fool

139. **RECLUSE** *(n.)*—A person who leads a secluded or solitary life

140. **CLAIRVOYANT** *(n.)*—Having the supposed power to see objects and events that cannot be perceived with the five traditional senses **CLAIRVOYANT** *(adj.)*—Having the ability to see into the future or beyond the normal senses

141. **PRODIGY** *(n.)*—A person with great talent; a young genius

142. **MISANTHROPE** *(n.)*—A person who hates or distrusts humankind

CHAPTER 6: SCIENCE CAN BE SOCIAL

143. **CONJECTURE** *(n.)*—An inference based upon guesswork; a supposition

144. **OBSOLETE, ARCHAIC, ANTIQUATED** *(adj.)*—No longer in use; outmoded in design or style

145. **PROTOTYPE** *(n.)*—An original model; an initial design

146. **FUTILE** *(adj.)*—Completely useless; doomed to failure; in vain

147. **INDIGENOUS, ENDEMIC** *(adj.)*—Native to an area

148. **PANDEMIC** *(n.)*—An epidemic that is geographically widespread and affects a large proportion of the population

149. **ADROIT, DEFT, DEXTEROUS** *(adj.)*—Having or showing great skill; nimble; **ADEPT** (DH Essential)

150. **SQUANDER** *(v.)*—To spend thoughtlessly; to waste

151. **INCONTROVERTIBLE** *(adj.)*—Impossible to deny or disprove; demonstrably true

152. **CONVOLUTED** *(adj.)*—Winding, twisting, and, therefore, difficult to understand; intricate

153. **PLACID, SERENE** *(adj.)*—Calm or quiet; undisturbed by tumult or disorder

154. **VIABLE, FEASIBLE** *(adj.)*—Capable of being accomplished; possible

155. **DISPARITY** *(n.)*—An inequality; a gap; an imbalance

156. **CURTAIL** *(v.)*—To cut short or reduce

157. **INNOCUOUS** *(adj.)*—Harmless; unlikely to give offense or to arouse strong feelings or hostility

158. **DIATRIBE, TIRADE, HARANGUE** *(n.)*—A bitter abusive denunciation; a thunderous verbal attack

159. **PARTISAN** *(n.)*—A supporter of a person, party, or cause; a person with strong and perhaps biased beliefs

160. **PROGNOSTICATOR** *(n.)*—A person who makes predictions based upon current information and data

161. **DICTATOR** *(n.)*—A person exercising absolute power, especially a ruler who has absolute, unrestricted control in a government

162. **PATRON, BENEFACTOR** (DH Essential) *(n.)*—A person who makes a gift or bequest
BENEFICIARY *(n.)*—The recipient of funds, titles, property, and other benefits

163. **PROPONENT, ADVOCATE** *(n.)*—One who argues in support of something; a champion of a cause

164. **INNOVATOR** *(n.)*—A person who introduces something new

165. **STOIC, STOLID** *(adj.)*—Seemingly **INDIFFERENT** (Word 113) to or unaffected by joy, grief, pleasure, or pain; impassive and emotionless

166. **REPROBATE** *(n.)*—A morally unprincipled person

CHAPTER 7: POP WORDS!

167. **AMBIVALENT** *(adj.)*—Having mixed or opposing feelings at the same time

168. **ANOMALY** *(n.)*—Deviation from the norm or what is expected
ANOMALOUS, ATYPICAL *(adj.)*—full of ANOMALIES

169. **PAUCITY** *(n.)*—A scarcity or shortage of something; **DEARTH** (DH Essential)

170. **PRATTLE** *(v.)*—To speak in a foolish manner; to babble incessantly

171. **UNCONVENTIONAL, UNORTHODOX** *(adj.)*—Not ordinary or typical; characterized by avoiding customary conventions and behaviors

172. **METICULOUS, PAINSTAKING, FASTIDIOUS** *(adj.)*—Extremely careful; very exacting

173. **DIFFIDENT, SELF-EFFACING** *(adj.)*—Hesitant due to a lack of self-confidence; unassertive; shy; retiring

174. **PRESUMPTUOUS** *(adj.)*—Taking liberties; brashly overstepping one's place; impertinently bold

175. **CLANDESTINE, SURREPTITIOUS** *(adj.)*—Secret; covert; not open; not aboveboard

176. **AMBIGUITY** *(n.)*—The quality or state of having more than one possible meaning; doubtful; **EQUIVOCAL** (Word 26)
AMBIGUOUS *(adj.)*—Unclear; uncertain; open to more than one interpretation; not definitive; **DUBIOUS** (DH Essential)

177. **REPROACH, CASTIGATE** *(n.)*—To express disapproval; to scold; to rebuke

178. **NOSTALGIA** *(n.)*—A **WISTFUL** (Word 17) sentimental longing for a place or time in the past
NOSTALGIC *(adj.)*—Experiencing or exhibiting **NOSTALGIA**

179. **GAFFE** *(n.)*—A blunder; a faux pas; a clumsy social or diplomatic error

180. **ANTITHESIS** *(n.)*—The direct or exact opposite; extreme contrast
ANTITHETICAL *(adj.)*—Exactly opposite

181. **ANTECEDENT, FORERUNNER** *(n.)*—A preceding event; something that comes before another

182. **IMPLAUSIBLE** *(adj.)*—Unbelievable; incredible; not **PLAUSIBLE** (DH Essential)

183. **ACQUIESCE** *(v.)*—To comply; to agree; to give in

184. **NAÏVE, GULLIBLE** *(adj.)*—Unaffectedly simple; lacking worldly expertise; unsophisticated; immature; inexperienced; **INGENUOUS** (DH Advanced)

185. **UBIQUITOUS, PREVALENT, PERVASIVE** *(adj.)*—Characterized by being everywhere; omnipresent; widespread

186. **DIMINUTIVE** *(adj.)*—Very small

187. **TRIVIAL** *(adj.)*—Trifling; unimportant; insignificant
MINUTIAE *(n.)*—Minor everyday details

188. **EXHORT** *(v.)*—To encourage; to urge; to give a pep talk; to **IMPLORE** (DH Essential)

189. **ANTIPATHY, ENMITY, RANCOR** *(n.)*—Strong dislike; ill will; the state of detesting someone

190. **DIGRESS** *(v.)*—To depart from a subject; to wander; to ramble

191. **TENACIOUS** *(adj.)*—Characterized by holding fast to something valued; showing great determination

192. **INDULGENT** *(adj.)*—Characterized by excessive generosity; overly tolerant

193. **EPHEMERAL, FLEETING, EVANESCENT** *(adj.)*—Very brief; lasting for a short time; transient
PERENNIAL *(adj.)*—Returning year after year; enduring

194. **PENCHANT, PREDILECTION, PROPENSITY** *(n.)*—A liking or preference for something; a **BENT** (DH Advanced); an inclination

195. **CAPRICIOUS, MERCURIAL, FICKLE** *(adj.)*—Very changeable; characterized by constantly shifting moods

196. **BOORISH, UNCOUTH, CRASS** *(adj.)*—Vulgar; characterized by crude behavior and deplorable manners; unrefined

197. **INNUENDO** *(n.)*—A veiled reference; an insinuation

198. **VORACIOUS, RAVENOUS, INSATIABLE** *(adj.)*—Having a huge appetite that cannot be satisfied

199. **POIGNANT** *(adj.)*—Moving; touching; heartrending

200. **DISPEL** *(v.)*—To drive away; scatter, as to **DISPEL** a misconception

201. **INTEMPERATE** *(adj.)*—Lacking restraint; excessive
TEMPERATE *(adj.)*—Exercising moderation and restraint

202. **LAUD, EXTOL, TOUT, ACCLAIM** *(v.)*—To praise; to applaud

203. **DISPARAGE** *(v.)*—To speak of in a slighting or disrespectful way; to belittle

204. **MENTOR** *(n.)*—An advisor; a teacher; a guide
ACOLYTE *(n.)*—A devoted follower

205. **BUNGLER** *(n.)*—Someone who is clumsy or **INEPT**; a person who makes mistakes because of incompetence
INEPT *(adj.)*—Incompetent, clumsy, or careless; having or showing no skill

206. **PUNDIT** *(n.)*—An expert commentator; an **AUTHORITY** (DH Essential) who expresses his or her opinion, usually on political issues

207. **NEOPHYTE, GREENHORN** *(n.)*—A beginner; someone new to a field or activity; **NOVICE** (DH Essential)

Answer Keys

CHAPTER 1

1. satire
2. eulogy
3. hyperbole
4. saga
5. synopsis

 CHAPTER 2

Answers will vary. Refer back to the word and definition to check your work. When you draw a word, make sure the image is vivid and/or humorous so that you will remember it easily!

CHAPTER 3

1. precarious
2. eccentric
3. redundant
4. irreverent
5. copious

6. rejuvenated
7. denounced
8. circumvent
9. extricated
10. rebuffed

CHAPTER 4

Answers will vary. Refer back to the word and definition to check your work. When you draw a word, make sure the image is vivid and/or humorous so that you will remember it easily.

 # CHAPTER 5

Unoriginal:	Characteristic of the charming countryside:
Word 1: trite	Word 1: bucolic
Word 2: banal	Word 2: rustic
Word 3: insipid	Word 3: pastoral

Answers may vary for definitions and synonyms

CHAPTER 6

1. innovator
2. curtail
3. obsolete
4. adroit
5. feasible
6. partisan
7. placid
8. squander
9. futile
10. dictator

CHAPTER 7

Extremely careful:	Characterized by crude behavior:
Word 1: meticulous	Word 1: boorish
Word 2: painstaking	Word 2: uncouth
Word 3: fastidious	Word 3: crass

Answers may vary for definitions and synonyms

INDEX